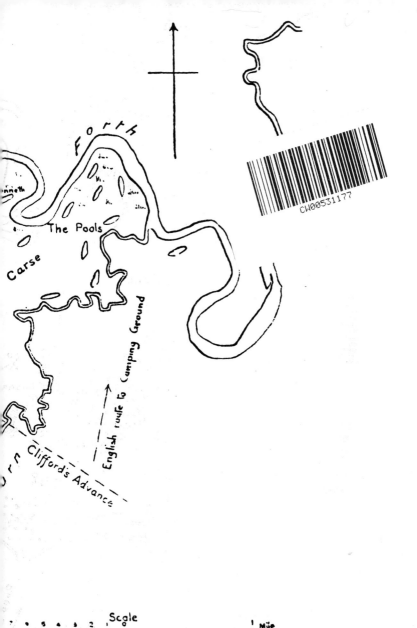

F o r t h

The Pools

Carse

English route to Camping Ground

Clifford's Advance

Scale

2   1   Mile

...sh Army approaching
...ough the Torwood

SUNDAY, JUNE 23.

...features are diagrammatic.

THE BATTLE OF BANNOCKBURN

PUBLISHED BY

JAMES MACLEHOSE AND SONS, GLASGOW,

Publishers to the University.

———

MACMILLAN AND CO., LTD., LONDON.

New York, - - The Macmillan Co.
Toronto, - - - The Macmillan Co. of Canada.
London, - - - Simpkin, Hamilton and Co.
Cambridge, - - Bowes and Bowes.
Edinburgh, - - Douglas and Foulis.
Sydney, - - - Angus and Robertson.

———

MCMXIII.

The
Battle of Bannockburn

A Study in Mediaeval Warfare

By

W. M. Mackenzie, M.A.

THE STRONG OAK PRESS

ISBN: 1-871048-03-6

Publishing History: This work was first published in 1913.
This edition reproduces the original text and plans complete
and unabridged.

Published by:

The Strong Oak Press
PO Box 47
Stevenage
Herts   SG2 8UH

Printed in Great Britain by Antony Rowe Ltd, Chippenham

PREFACE

In the following pages I have told the story of the Bannockburn campaign, with a brief survey of the related events and conditions that brought it to pass. It is not an exhaustive treatise for several reasons; because it was desirable to confine the book to a small scale, because I wished to stress the central thesis and keep the issues clear, and because there are handicaps of a personal nature to such a performance. At the same time, the frequent suggestions from several quarters to make my analysis and conclusions more accessible in a compact form have rendered something of the sort necessary.

The kernel of the book is an elaboration of a paper which I read to the Glasgow Archaeological Society, and which is published in their *Transactions* of 1910. That, in turn, was the outcome of studies in *The Bruce* and other fourteenth-century literature, and in my edition of that poem (Black, 1909) an even fuller analysis of portions of some of the matter may be found, the necessities being different from the present. Several personal examinations of the ground have contributed to my conviction.

My account will be found to differ radically from that generally accepted, but is claimed to be, in every particular, based upon the contemporary material. Adequate references have therefore been supplied, and it is upon these that my case or any case must rest. It is no pleasant duty to differ from the conclusions of those for whose work generally one has the profoundest respect. That my account exhibits the two days' fighting at Bannockburn as an even more remarkable and significant episode in its characteristics than has hitherto been assumed, and raises the generalship of Bruce to a conspicuous height in mediaeval warfare, will not, I am sure, be accounted a preliminary objection.

I am the more encouraged by the appreciation and adherence of others whose qualifications in the historic field are beyond cavil. Particularly I am grateful to Professor Tout, whose name is sufficient for historic students. "Revolutionary" he confesses my reading to be, but adds, I am permitted to say, that, in his opinion, my article suggests the "right solution of the problem of the tactics of Bannockburn." In his recent Ford Lectures at Oxford he has committed himself to the same judgment.

My position being such I have tried to avoid rhetoric, to be as clear and straightforward in my statements as one can be, to establish every point, and to invite critical frankness by using the same freedom. I am really concerned, in view of the coming centennial, to give an opening for a careful overhaul of the data, and to have the whole thing thrashed out as it ought to be. I await the result with confidence :

> Tharfor I wald fayne set my will,
> Giff my wyt mycht suffice thartill,
> To put in wryt a suthfast story.

W. M. M.

CONTENTS

CHAPTER I.

GENERAL STRATEGY OF THE WAR.

FOR six years, since on the shore of the Solway
Edward I. "eased his restless heart and ruth-
less hand," Robert Bruce, with capable lieu-
tenants and an adventurous following, had been
methodically casting off the shackles of English
domination in Scotland. Very different were
the circumstances from those which had presented themselves to William Wallace in the
spring of 1297. A sudden, wrathful flame of
revolt, the signal and clever triumph at Stirling
Bridge and a sweeping movement over the
Lowlands, had then sufficed to clear the country
of the invader. But when the grip was once
again secured, it was made more firm and
systematic.

The land bristled with garrisoned castles and
fortified posts : the fetters were set fully on.

A   1

THE BATTLE OF BANNOCKBURN

As Scotland is divided into several geographical areas, and there is no central strategic locality for the country as a whole, fortifications had to be numerous, and mainly ranged along the great natural highways. Resistance, however united and sustained, had been worn down, and hope crushed even out of the most strenuous. But clement as the conqueror had been in his hour of victory, all the fury and cruelty of a masterful nature suddenly pierced to the quick of its confidence and complacency, flashed out at the revolt of the Earl of Carrick, a man forsworn, a sacrilegious assassin ; and a moral orgy of unscrupulous onslaught, as on a criminal and his accomplices, of swift punishment and death with every circumstance of infamy, seemed to have shattered to pieces the latest exhibition of national effrontery.

The first frantic stroke of Bruce, the murder of John Comyn, had, moreover, brought to the English side the ally of a family vendetta within the country itself. Yet from his harried haunt among his native hills of Carrick and Galloway, whither wronged and resentful men were steadily stealing to his company, Bruce, in the early summer of 1307, struck one sharp and significant stroke at Loudoun Hill that rang through Scotland. The death of Edward a month later was a fateful advantage for the cause of " King Hobbe." At last the occasion had come upon which the Bruce intrigue had based its hopes,[1] an intrigue so foolishly compromised and almost destroyed by his premature and impulsive action.

But the hold of the dead man's hand was hard on Scotland. Strongholds and fortified towns kept Bruce and his bands to the open country. It was his first task to ensure that there at least he could move easily about and strike as it pleased him. Generally he could count on sympathy and even support, restrained mainly by the neighbourhood of garrisons or exposure to English reprisals ; for, though many Scots were on the other side and families were divided, it was mostly but a shallow allegiance motived by fear or prudence ; "their hearts," the English chronicler confesses, "if not their

[1] *Scalacronica* (Maitland Club), p. 130.

bodies, were always with their own people."[1]
The officials of the occupation, too, by harshly
exploiting their opportunities to their private
gain, were educating recruits for revolt.

But in the territories where the Comyn interest
had sway, particularly in Galloway, the larger
cause was drowned in jealousy and hate. Fortunately these territories were widely separated
from each other, could not locally co-operate,
and thus could be mastered in detail. Bruce
himself wasted Buchan in a fashion that left a
shuddering memory for half a century, and the
Comyn who was its earl had to find a refuge in
England. The same fate, in their turn, over-
took the Macdougalls of Lorn, who found no
friends among the Argyllshire chiefs.[2] Galloway
had been heavily hammered by the two Bruces
and Douglas on more than one occasion—in the
autumn following the success of Loudoun Hill,
and again in the year after, when many of the

---

[1] *Chronicon de Lanercost* (Maitland Club), p. 217.

[2] Bain's *Calendar*, iii. No. 80. On the attitude of the High-
landers and Islesmen of the west, cf. next note. The anti-
national section there was a special case, the outcome of the
Comyn blood-feud.

local gentry were slain and others of the people driven across the border.[1] As this district flanked what was to be King Robert's favourite line of advance into England, it was a further necessity that its hostility should be made ineffective.

For the next stage in the development of Bruce's general strategy finds him taking the aggressive in a series of attacks upon northern England. There is, indeed, an interval from the midsummer of 1310 to that of 1311 when Edward II. is constantly at the front in the north. In the former year he brings an army into Scotland, leads it across the Lowlands, up Tweeddale by Peebles, through the Biggar gap into Clydesdale and round Glasgow to the base selected by his father in the peel of Linlithgow— a strategic cross-country route in the Scottish wars. He found no "rebels" in his path; Bruce kept to his "caves and woods," emerging only to pick up foraging parties away from the main

[1] *Lanercost*, pp. 210, 212. In 1308 the leaders were Edward Bruce, Alexander Lindsay, Robert Boyd and James Douglas, and it is significant that their following was from the outer isles. Cf. also *Foedera*, iii. p. 14.

body, or to punish English loyalists in Lothian when Edward retired upon Berwick.[1]

In February, 1311, an English column traversed the country up to beyond Perth, making a further parade of "the King's peace," entrapping unfortunate people to a submission in which they could not be protected. Edward himself had passed the winter in Scotland, but his mind was distracted by another problem.[2] For once more, as in the first Edward's time, the game of politics in England was being played to the advantage of the Scots. The English barons were really more concerned in getting rid of his foreign friend, Piers Gaveston, than in crushing Bruce. During all the years of the struggle against both Edwards, the political cabals against these kings were a most serious hampering of their efforts at conquest. Pride of victory apart, the English baronage was never whole-hearted in the Scottish affair. As between a political triumph at home and a

[1] *Vita Edwardi Secundi*, in *Chronicles, Edward I. and Edward II.* ii. p. 165 ; *Lanercost*, p. 214.

[2] *Lanercost*, p. 214.

6

triumph in Scotland they always made their choice of the former.[1]   Thus it was a clear gain for the Scottish nationalists that the most active and conspicuous of the column commanders on this occasion should just be Gaveston, Earl of Cornwall, so that the campaign came to a summary conclusion when the English earls took in hand to make an end of him.   The way was then open for Bruce to resume his aggressive operations, and the same year and the succeeding years saw him conducting or directing destructive raids upon the four northern English shires, sacking their towns, even Durham itself, lifting their cattle, and holding his hand only on payment of heavy sums, not less than £2000 a time from a shire, for immunity during a term of months; until, it was computed, he had in all exacted a sum of not less than £40,000,[2] or

[1] *Vita Edwardi*, p. 167.   The *Lanercost* writer (p. 212) says that even Edward himself was prepared to combine with Bruce against his barons.   In *Vita Edwardi* he is represented as willing to barter the freedom of Scotland for protection to Piers Gaveston, but Bruce flatly refused to trust his promises (p. 175). Other references to Bruce taking advantage of baronial opposition in *Lanercost*, p. 216 (1311), p. 219 (1312).

[2] *Lanercost*, pp. 217, 220 ; *Vita Edw.* p. 199.   *Lanercost* says Edward Bruce was in Cumberland in April, 1314.

7

nearly half a million in modern values; thus paying his army as Napoleon paid "the army of Italy," and spoiling the Egyptians to replenish his exchequer. In like fashion he extorted tribute from the Anglified district of the Lothians. On the other hand, the English garrisons were securing the local revenues from the Scottish districts which they commanded, though one can guess that, when upkeep was considered, the gain in this system of contra-accounts was not on their side. And northern England was meantime wholly demoralised in a military sense.

It had been the gibe of English song-writers in the early days that "King Hobbe" kept himself to the moors and came not to town, with contemptuous threats of what would happen if he did. By this time, however, King Hobbe or Bob, with a record of steady success behind him and, in consequence, a largely increased following, free of the uplands and with money in his purse, was coming to town and castle, and in no beggarly fashion either. The final and hardest labour was to tear up the roots of

8

the English occupation by getting rid of the garrisons and, as his policy was, destroying all strongholds, a policy of providing no foothold for the invader which was to become a principle in Scottish military practice.[1]

It was an age in which fortified positions were, out of all proportion, stronger than even the best directed attack. In the spring of 1304 the reducing of Stirling Castle had occupied Edward with his whole field force and every requisite, including thirteen siege engines, for three months; and yet the starved-out garrison which then surrendered, after losses which do not seem to have been heavy, numbered only some more than a hundred and forty.[2] Fortifications were of two great classes, apart from the natural advantage of a site. There was the castle of high stone walls and towers, of which Bothwell on the Clyde in part remains as an impressive example, with a deep ditch where possible or necessary. And there was the more

[1] See my paper on "Scotland's Historic National Defence" in *Proceedings of Glasgow Philos. Socy.* 1913.

[2] Hemingburgh, *Chronicon*, ii. p. 232.

easily and quickly constructed "peel," of which the naming feature was the tall wooden palisade, also with its ditch; the palisade, too, usually set upon an earthen mound. In such wise were the principal towns of Scotland fortified,[1] though Edward I. had started to give Berwick a stone wall, and Perth, by one account, was unique in being so provided.[2] It scarcely consists with this that, at the beginning of the insurrection, the burgesses of the city had, by English instructions, equipped it with a peel and fosse or ditch.[3]

But either type of passive defence, well garrisoned with men-at-arms, archers and crossbowmen, and adequately provisioned, was a terribly hard nut to crack. An average castle garrison would not much exceed a hundred fighting men, and twice as many would be rare. Lochmaben, an important strategical point on the Annandale route, contained in 1313 fourteen

[1] *Chronique de Jean le Bel*, i. chap. xxii. : "Les plus grosses villes fermées de bons fossez et de bons palis"—the largest towns enclosed with good ditches and palisades.

[2] Barbour's *Bruce*, bk. ix. 335-6.

[3] Bain's *Calendar*, iii. No. 68.

men-at-arms—knights and squires and one light
horseman or "hobelar"—sixty-five archers, five
crossbowmen in the castle and twenty in the
peel.[1] Yet Lochmaben held out among the
very last, though Edward Bruce had been
rampaging for years through Galloway, and, if
we may believe Barbour, had a scoop of thirteen
castles to his credit in a single twelvemonth.
These must have been small places, the *castella*
in which the province was rich, or, at any
rate, isolated by the circumstances and easily
blockaded, so that the garrisons surrendered
from starvation, or were so demoralised, for the
same reasons, as to be soon rushed. Certainly
in 1312 Sir Dougal Macdouall was complaining
from the castle of Dumfries that he was being
neglected in the matter of provisions, and that
his men were consequently deserting.[2] In
February of the year after he had to surrender
the place. The garrisons, of course, were waged
men, professional soldiers, captains with bands
of troopers—Bruce's old enemy, Aymer de
Valence, Earl of Pembroke, served as such a

[1] Bain, No. 336.   [2] Bain, No. 281.

commander—and companies of archers and crossbowmen, whose maintenance was a heavy burden on the English exchequer. Many of these mercenaries were foreigners: a Burgundian was constable of Roxburgh Castle, a Gascon of Edinburgh.

Now to capture each of these places by a regular siege would be a wearisome and uncertain enterprise. Bruce had little to lay out on siege artillery, and he could not afford to have his men tied down for lengthy periods to single situations. Mobility was his strategic weapon. He might starve them out, for their flour and bacon and dried fish were bound to run short or go bad, but that, too, took up precious time, and there was always the possible distraction of a relief. It was a case in which brains must be matched against stolid resistance.

And there was a weakness at another point besides food-supply, in the poor watch kept. Watchmen or sentinels were hired as such like the rest: Lochmaben had only one, but usually there were more. To neglect of watch was attributed the fall of Forfar Castle, when a local friend of the king climbed the wall at night.[1] The same was said of Perth town, which fell to a night surprise by Bruce himself.[2] Thus a favourite Scottish siege weapon was a specially constructed rope-ladder for a night assault.[3] The strong and important post of Roxburgh was climbed into, on a night of feasting, by James Douglas and the men who, under black cloaks, had crawled up to the walls; the watchmen having taken them for the usual little black cattle foolishly left out. Linlithgow had been entered by the not uncommon trick of blocking the entrance with a waggon of hay, in which was concealed part of a force hidden near by. Edinburgh rock was scaled while the garrison was kept occupied with an attack in front. There never were enough men in a fortress to

---

[1] *The Bruce*, ix. 318.   [2] *Lanercost*, p. 222.

[3] Such ladders are described by the *Lanercost* writer as used by the Scots in the unsuccessful night attack on Berwick in 1312. They were of the height of the wall, were knotted at intervals of a foot and a half to bear wooden steps, and had a specially constructed hook to hold on at the top. In this crooked iron plate was a hole for a spear, upon which two men could lift the ladder and set it on the wall. Berwick was saved by the barking of a dog (p. 221, *V.E.* p. 200).

hold the whole line of defences, since an all-round attack was rarely possible. Although dates are not always certain, Perth, Dumfries and Linlithgow are captures of 1313; Roxburgh and Edinburgh of February and March, 1314. It is over the operations at Stirling that the chief difficulty arises.

The English account is that Stirling Castle was assailed by Robert Bruce immediately after the successes at Roxburgh and Edinburgh; on the Scottish side it is said that Edward Bruce had been engaged in the siege from Lent till midsummer, 1313.[1] Both agree that it was the failure of provisions that made its governor, Sir Philip Mowbray, enter into a compact to surrender the place by June 24, 1314, unless by that time an army had come to his relief. This sort of bargain is fairly familiar; James IV. got Norham before Flodden on the same terms, though there it was only a matter of days. The English writer affirms that Mowbray was reporting this understanding to Edward II. at the beginning of Lent, 1314, with the additional

[1] *Vita Edw.* p. 200; *Bruce*, x. 813-6.

news of the fate of the other castles. This is scarcely possible chronologically.

On the other hand, it is clear that in November, 1313, Edward was already contemplating an advance into Scotland at the following midsummer,[1] the most convenient time of the year, since by that date the grass would be sufficiently grown to feed the great array of horses that would accompany any campaign—an imperative consideration for early campaigning in a country depending solely on its coarse native fodder.[2] The net result is the same. By June 24, 1314, Stirling Castle must be "rescued by battle," or it was pledged to surrender. Edward, moved almost to tears at hearing how these noble castles were not only captured but destroyed,[3] or rendered untenable, had made up his mind to strike a blow which should not merely relieve Stirling but finally crush the Scottish insurrection. Thus Stirling Castle became the stake which should bring about the collision of the national forces.

[1] *Foedera*, iii. p. 463 ; Bain, No. 337.
[2] *Lanercost*, p. 214.   [3] *Vita Edw.* p. 200.

15

We can well believe, if the compact was really the work of his brother Edward, that it did not meet with the approval of King Robert; the risk was so great. It was no part of his strategy to allow himself to be brought face to face with the armed forces of England in the field, where the chances would all run in favour of the enemy, so greatly superior in numbers and equipment. The meeting would have consequences, material and, what was even more serious, moral, which would almost make it final. It would mean not so much Scotland as England at bay, and that was no light or hopeful vision.

The date fixed upon connects with a circumstance already noted; an English army did not willingly venture into Scotland until the horses could be sure of provender, and that was not until the beginning of June at earliest. This was one of the special difficulties of campaigning. Mountain refuges, wooded tracks and frequent marshy ground were permanent fixtures of defence,[1] but no less was the imperfect

---

[1] In *Vita Edw.* Bruce and his men, during the operations of 1310, are described as secluded "in caves and wooded places"

character of Scottish tillage. An army could not even depend on feeding itself in the country, for the line of march could be cleared of supplies, hence the frequent use of a commissariat column in the shape of a fleet, which in turn was at the mercy of the winds ; but the feeding of the crowd of horses was an even more critical question. A strong horse, in good condition, was essential to the heavily armoured feudal warrior; it was the last resort of a garrison, with food fast running short, to eat their horses. On the occasions on which Edward I. wintered in Scotland he ran serious risks in lack of horse forage. During his stay in Linlithgow in the winter of 1300-1 he lost a heavy tale of horses partly by starvation.[1] Edward II. once tried a March campaign (1311) and had

(*in speluncis et locis nemorosis*, p. 165). Next year while the English army perambulates the kingdom he is inaccessible in "places mountainous, pathless, marshy" (*loca montana, invia, aquosa*, p. 167). The Scots flying from Gaveston, Earl of Cornwall, "had their retreats always in mountains and marshes" (*in montibus et moriscis sua semper receptacula habuerunt*, Hemingburgh, ii. p. 278).

[1] "Through lack of forage and the winter cold" (*propter defectum foragii et frigoris hiemalis.* Hemingburgh, ii. p. 222).

hurriedly to abandon it for the same reason.[1] All these conditions, too, added heavily to the sheer expense of the war, necessitating the maintenance throughout the year of paid garrisons and their supply. Thus, too, by fixing the date of the coming engagement at midsummer, the passive advantage of climatic and pastoral drawbacks had to be foregone; and June of this week,[2] 1314, was dry. Only in a summer month was a "Bannockburn" possible.

[1] Hemingburgh, p. 278.   [2] Cf. *Bruce*, xi. 616.

CHAPTER II.

THE ARMIES, COMMANDERS AND LINE
OF MARCH.

As we have seen, Edward II. was already contemplating a movement in force upon Scotland
for the summer of 1314, no doubt in order to
check the closing in upon the castles, the stage
which Bruce's strategy had reached. These gone
all was gone. But Bruce had acted with greater
speed and success than he could have thought
possible. Winter had always been the Scottish
season for effective work; it was a maxim of
the War of Independence that if the country
was to be conquered it must be done in the
winter ;[1] a principle which Edward I. had found
to apply also to the case of Wales, and which he
had used in Scotland when possible, and only
then with any cumulative success. Otherwise,

---

[1] *Lanercost*, pp. 202, 287.

under the immunity of a season unsuitable and untimely for regular feudal campaigning, lost ground was recovered by tenacious foes more independent of mere weather conditions. For this reason and those already given, all frequently illustrated in the Scottish wars, winter operations by an English host were normally impracticable; hence Bruce's bursts of activity in autumn and early spring.

As so often, too, political conditions even now threatened to hamper Edward's purpose. When he expressed to his earls his desire to proceed at once to drive out the traitor who was making himself king, their answer was that the matter should first come before Parliament, to which he objected that this meant delay when immediate action was necessary. In this he was supported by his personal advisers and friends. He need ask for no money for paid troops; they pointed out that by simply exacting what was due in feudal military service he could make such a muster as would put Scottish resistance out of count. Even if some barons did not provide their

following it mattered not. Gloucester and
Pembroke and Hereford and Robert de Clifford
and Hugh Despenser and the permanent military establishment of the royal household could
be depended on, and this of itself sufficed.[1] In
fact the Earls of Lancaster, Warenn, Arundel
and Warwick did not join the army, though
they provided the contingents for which they
were liable. On these lines, therefore, and in
this spirit Edward set about making his preparations. Pembroke, appointed Guardian of Scotland, was sent forward with a detachment to
keep an eye upon any tricky contrivances of
the Scots and clear the way for his royal
master ;[2] he had had a good deal of experience
in work of this kind.

II.

Pembroke's mission, however, seems to have
been connected with a proposed Easter campaign, most elaborate preparations for which

[1] *Vita Edw.* pp. 200-1.

[2] *Ibid.* p. 201 ; *Foedera*, iii. No. 477. But his commission is
dated March 24.

fill many pages of the rolls,[1] but which after all did not come off. Its objective is in general terms—the king's rebels of Scotland. But there is precise reference to the serious position of Stirling two months later when the call for service went forth to the barons for their mounted contingents, and to the sheriffs of shires, the lords of the Welsh marches and Wales itself for levies of foot. Wark, well up the Tweed on the English side, and near the ford at Coldstream, was given as the place of muster, and Monday, June 10, as the date; but the army is said actually to have started from Berwick on June 17 or 18.[2] The rendezvous at Wark,[3] however, and consideration of the route taken, which will be noticed later, may perhaps qualify this statement, though no doubt it holds true for the king and his personal entourage.

Of the number of men who thus assembled, we have no certain statement. The Scottish

[1] *Rot. Scotiae*, pp. 114 ff. *Parlt. Writs*, vol. ii. div. 1, p. 112.

[2] *Vita Edw.* p. 201; *Bruce*, xi. 136, 184. Barbour makes them assemble at, and start from, Berwick.

[3] *Foedera*, iii. No. 482.

chroniclers alone give a total estimate, but great exaggeration in numbers disfigures all the chronicles of the time, English or Scottish, particularly when dealing with the forces of an enemy. Abbot Bernard of Arbroath wrote a contemporary poem on the battle in which he credits the English with 3100 horse and 40,000 foot.[1] On the whole, for a writer of that time, this is not so bad. It is a vastly soberer estimate than that of John Barbour, who affirms that Edward had more than 100,000 fighting men,[2] made up of 3000 heavily armoured horsemen on armoured horses, as part of a full cavalry corps of 40,000 men-at-arms, 50,000 archers and a remainder of light horsemen or "hobblers" and common foot. How greatly exaggerated this is, a very little analysis will show.

The total number of knights' fees in England, that is units of land owing the service of

[1] *Scotichronicon* (ed. 1759), ii. chap. xxi. p. 248.

[2] Barbour's practice, where he had no other data, seems to have been to guess 10,000 to a battalion, as a sort of conventional figure for a very great number (cf. Latin use of *sexcenti* in same way). He says as much in one case, xiv 258, 270. There five "battles" are "to ges" 50,000 : here ten are 100,000.

one knight, has been calculated by one investi-
gator at 5000, by another has been more
liberally raised to something nearer 7000.[1]
In the present case, however, these figures
can serve only as a warning not as a guide.
For reasons which need not be discussed the
custom of a fixed quota had taken the place of
the old calculation by fees. Thus Gloucester,
holding 455 fees, was responsible for only ten
knights; Norfolk with 211 fees for five knights.
Inferiors might make up their due of knights
in fractions representing men of inferior equipment. And, indeed, to every quota of knights
proper—the fully armoured man on the armoured
horse—may be added on the average at least
twice the number of these inferior troopers,
roughly distinguished by a less complete
personal equipment and a horse too light to
carry armour of its own in addition to an
armoured rider.[2] Even so, a slight reflection
will show how the total number of effective

[1] J. H. Round, *Feudal England*, p. 292 ; J. E. Morris in
Welsh Wars of Edward I. p. 41 : cf. throughout and see
Appendix C in my edition of *The Bruce* (London, 1909).

[2] Morris, pp. 81-2.

cavalry must shrink. On these lines it has been concluded that the maximum of the cavalry arm in England might reach 8000, but every consideration is against the possibility of such a number being brought together at any time. For one thing sufficient mounts and remounts were certainly not available.

When we turn to actual figures we find Hemingburgh declaring that for Falkirk (1298) the English cavalry, when counted, came to 3000 on barded horses and about 4000 on uncovered horses, the distinction noted above. The first summation curiously corresponds with that of Barbour for the "helit (armoured or barded) horse" at Bannockburn.[1] But a calculation from the cavalry and other rolls runs down this 7000 to not more than 2400, and it is not certain that all these were present.[2] Now a contemporary English chronicler (c. 1325) fixes the number of men-at-arms who were in the Bannockburn army at over 2000; this while lauding the exceptional size

[1] *The Bruce*, xi. 106-7.
[2] Morris, p. 292.

and magnificence of the force.[1] His figure covers all the horsemen, for he adds on the other part an abundance of foot. And it must include not only the English chivalry but also dribblings of mounted soldiers from other countries, the four German knights who came for love[2] and the men from the French provinces, though not the hobblers or light horsemen on nags, who, as usual, probably formed part of the Irish contribution. Of course this chronicler may be patriotically diminishing, as Barbour under a like impulse was exaggerating, though the context would not bear this out; but his figure of 2000 and Abbot Bernard's of 3100 stand for the lower and upper limits of the number of English cavalry at Bannockburn.

Of the foot it might seem, at first sight, that

[1] *Vita Edw.* p. 201.

[2] *English Hist. Review*, vol. xix. p. 507. An additional portion of the Latin poem by Friar Baston, in the *Scoti-chronicon*, who accompanied the English army to celebrate its victory. It is too utterly rhetorical and conventional to yield any definite guidance. He was captured by the Scots, had to compose for them and said as little specific as he could, if the bulk of his poem was not in form beforehand.

a pretty close calculation could be made, for we have the precise number of the levies expected from the English counties and from Wales, as well as in respect of Ireland. That country, moreover, had long notice [1] and a fair muster might be expected, though here, too, there are contrary circumstances. They are mentioned by Barbour as a great company. But this might almost apply equally to the 361 Irish who came to Edward I.'s great army of 1300, or to the 3500 who were the maximum in the army of 1304. In the present case the Justiciar is required to raise 4000 archers and foot to be ready for embarkation on Whitsuntide next, May 26, to pass to Scotland in a fleet under John of Argyll. Probably the route was altered, but the figures may be accepted as a basis for calculation. It might be expected that the Welsh and Marches men, well used to fighting and its prizes, who were assessed at about 5000, would turn up pretty strong, but the

[1] Writ dated for issue March 28 ; *Pty. Writs*, ii. div. 1, p. 113; for English and Welsh, May 27 (*Foedera*, iii. No. 482). There is great risk of confusion between the summonses for Easter and June.

time allowed them, less than three weeks, to assemble and get to the Tweed was short enough. This latter consideration would affect also the levies from the more midland English counties, such as Warwick and Leicester. The shires to the south were not drawn upon; it was not yet the custom to do so for the Scottish wars, just as the northern counties would be exempt for a French war. In the present case, too, Cumberland and Westmoreland were left out; the Scots may have battered them too effectually. The foot from the dozen purely English shires should have come to 16,500 men, and the grand total of foot, excluding Irish and foreigners, to 21,540.[1]

But an important reservation must be made. So far as the round numbers of such levies go, the check of pay-rolls and obvious restrictions make us unwilling to accept them at their face value. Thus after Stirling Bridge the Earl of Surrey called out 29,000 foot from Wales and northern England to assemble at Newcastle

[1] *Foedera*, iii. No. 482; *Rotuli Scotiae*, i. p. 127; *Parl. Writs*, bk. ii. div. 1, p. 117.

by the last day of December. By February 9 only 16,000 had put in an appearance.[1] For the Caerlaverock campaign in 1300 Edward I. summoned 16,000 from seven northern shires. The highest figure, in July, ran to 7619, and it had been less than half as much.[2] On May 12, 1301, he ordered for midsummer, giving a much longer notice than was given for Bannockburn, 12,000 men from nine of the shires included in that list. But York, assessed as in the latter case at 4000, shows only 1193 on the pay-roll of early July, and Northumberland gives an exceptionally large proportion in 2019 out of 2700. Over all, however, the number then actually serving is only 5501, less than fifty per cent. of the nominal levy.[3]

All these data, then, work to the same conclusion, that not much more than half the full levy might be looked for. Tastes in estimates will vary, and some parts here must for ever remain guess-work; but if we accept the fair conclusion that a typical army of Edward I. in

[1] Morris, pp. 284-5.   [2] *Ibid.* p. 301.
[3] Bain's *Calendar*, ii. No. 1202, 1229.

his later years came to about 2000 horse and 10,000 foot,[1] with the foregoing analysis, and, relying on that, put the horse at the higher figure of 3000, accept less than two-thirds of the English and Welsh foot, or (say) 13,000 men, and expand with the other contingents the full numeration to 20,000 all told, we shall probably be not very far out, and shall have provided, under all the conditions of the time, a host sufficiently large to justify all the admiration which it received from both sides. The amount of military material required, the number of horses, including remounts, the baggage and victualling and disposition of so great a mass would strain even the resources of such a country as England was in comparison with Scotland.

Of the Scottish army it is even more difficult to arrive at a definite idea. Barbour states that it was more than thirty thousand strong, but we have seen how such estimates shrink in the cold light of records; it may be seen even in modern speculations as to the size of crowds :

[1] Morris, 229.

an English claim is for forty thousand. But even in Scotland's palmy days, and with the attraction of good pay, rarely did more than 20,000 men in all go to the front.[1]

At Halidon Hill in 1333 the Scots are declared to have had 1174 knights and men-at-arms and 13,500 light-armed footmen. According to Froissart, the Admiral of France, who came to Scotland in 1385, found that the army on service consisted of 500 horse and 30,000 foot. The horse may be pretty near the mark; it is the number Bruce is said to have retained at Bannockburn; the foot is always a careless item in feudal military analysis. For the Bannockburn case we must remember, too, that the whole country could not be drawn upon; the English could still claim a good body,[2] if not of active supporters, at least of prudent neutrals, probably in the Lothians for most, like the Border exposed to immediate retaliation. It is also in a small way indicative of the size

[1] Cf. for data my paper on "Scotland's Historic National Defence" in *Proceedings, Royal Phil. Socy. of Glasgow*, 1913.

[2] Bruce gives Edward 'a gret party' of Scotland (*Bruce*, xi. 46).

of the Scottish army that, after Moray's successful blow, almost all the fighting men crowded
round to congratulate him and were addressed
on the spot by Bruce himself. On the whole,
it is likely that Barbour's ratio, at least, is not
very far out, and that something near 7000
men will hold in the muster of Bruce. It
must be remembered that, up to now, his
force in the field, sustaining what was really
a guerilla warfare, cannot have amounted to
more than hundreds, and his full-size assemblage was clearly of effective, that is selected,
men ready to risk and dare.[1] He did not put
his trust in numbers ; on the contrary, he made
proclamation that any weak of courage should
depart in good time ; he wanted only men who
would stand to the end and "wyn all or de
with honour."[2]

It was this characteristic, with the experience
and encouragement of seven years of hard
struggle, that reduced the apparently heavy
chances against the Scots. By all rules and
paper calculations the English host should wipe

---

[1] *Bruce*, xi. 210-234.   [2] *Ibid.* xi. 397.

the Scots off the ground. And there was full confidence in such an outcome. That genera-tion had seen no more splendid army go out of England. It should have a walk-over; all Scotland gathered on the spot, according to the judgment of some, could not withstand it. The mass of horsemen alone, and it was in these that confidence was really placed, courageous men in all the appurtenances of feudal war, mail-clad and many further strengthened with plates in weak places, raised, like a living pro-jectile, with lance and axe and sword, on heavy shire horses also armoured, or on lighter but still strong mounts—could anything on foot, as the Scots were mainly bound to be, offer serious opposition to such a bombardment.

The lesson of Falkirk was forgotten. Then it was the archers and the generalship of Edward I. that had turned imminent disaster to victory. That the Flemish foot had shat-tered the chivalry of France at Courtrai twelve years before—that lesson was understood only when the time of explanations came. The tactical problem of the period was the combining

E   33

of horse and foot, of lance and bow, in the operations of the field, and in that respect no advance had been made since the day of Falkirk, and even that example was disregarded. The great gap between horse and foot was still unbridged. The latter could scarcely be called even a second line. If the horse were repulsed, all were repulsed, and mere footmen were grain for the red reaper of victory. They were conscious of this, and, in the event of a losing game, panic was sure to come soon and irresistibly.

It was not so with the Scots. With the exception of their little band of horse, whose duty was limited to a special end, they were an army of infantry. They took equal chances. Every man could feel himself a factor, a fair unit in the fight. Every man had some amount of light armour, sufficient to meet sword-cuts, with an axe by his side for close conflict, and a long pike.[1] This equalising of chances and importance, and homogeneity of armament, while making for mobility, simplified the hand-

[1] *Vita Edw.* p. 203.

ling of masses of men, and gave an equal interest to all. It was a simple democratic army against a twin but unjointed feudal assemblage.

III.

Withal there was on the Scottish side experience and trained military skill. Of Douglas's contingent it is specially noted that they had the advantage of being well used to fighting ; but in every brigade there was at least a stiffening of veterans. On the part of their foes the English peasantry were still inferior material, of whom the men of the Welsh marches and the Welsh themselves, from a life of bickering, were usually accounted the most useful. At Falkirk the bulk of Edward's foot was from Wales. , But all alike suffered from knightly disregard. Moreover, Edward II., with those aesthetic leanings so fatal to a feudal monarch, was no soldier. Nor had his leading officers any particular gifts ; the feudal knight had courage in plenty, but rarely would deign to use art.

It mattered less here, because Edward refused such advice as was offered him. Sir Ingram de Umfraville, of the house of Angus, drawing on his knowledge of the Scot was to proffer some, to have it contemptuously brushed aside. The Earl of Gloucester was only twenty-four, and had seen little service. Hereford, the Constable, was also young, and Gloucester and he seem to have been unable to forget their family rivalries even in face of the enemy. Pembroke had done a good deal of active service in Scotland, as also had Sir Robert Clifford, but this was not the day of Pembroke's Methven trick; both were of the class of routine professional captains. Sir Giles de Argentine was a knight-errant in spirit as in fact, who had served as a squire in Wales, and had, as a good Crusader, slain his share of Saracens; he had a big sentimental reputation, but at Bannockburn saw no alternative save to get himself gloriously killed. Such independent action and lack of proper subordination were still the flaws of feudal warfare.

With the Scots, however, the commanders were clearly differentiated and recognised, as the

36

result of sheer military pressure and selection, and their marked individual qualities were wont to be used in co-operation, not in conflict. Robert Bruce had been stripped of his chivalric illusions; he had had a prolonged lessoning in the adaptation of his military means to his ends, been encouraged to act promptly, to read ground like Napoleon, and to draw upon every resource. His brother Edward was of more daring temper, to the verge and over of reck-lessness, and never understood the meaning of odds. But in a desperate cause such a per-sonality has its place. James Douglas was the Ulysses of the war; of infinite stratagems, but as skilful with his hands as with his head. Not a scar did that face ever show that had led the way in many a hard bout and assault. And Randolph, Earl of Moray, might be trusted effectually to do his share, though less mentally alert than his fellows. Years of common activity had given these men knowledge of each other's qualities and respect for them, and their reputa-tions were buttresses to the host.

But excellent as the group was, King Robert

himself, alike by his characteristics of heart and brain, held an unquestionable position, and was as much a captain to his men as to his officers. Hard circumstance had developed and given edge to what was most necessary in the Scottish leaders; in comparison, the English, equally brave and high-spirited, were but amateurs or of undeveloped talents, with a few veterans. It was bulk against brains; ambition against a cause; supreme and not unjustifiable self-confidence against men who were strong enough to fail and not weak enough to be suppressed.

IV.

It is necessary to say what can be said as to the route which the English army followed through Scotland, especially as we have all lightly assumed that this was by the Dunbar road on the eastern shore. Here it is well to remember not only men and horses, but the crowd of heavy, cumbersome, transport waggons carrying supplies for the host. Victuals there had to be in great quantity; a military Gargantua had to be fed, daintily, too, in the case of the gentlemen, for with them went table vessels of silver and gold or silver-gilt.[1]   Early in May Edward is ordering the diversion of all food-stuffs for sale to his army in Scotland; export elsewhere is barred.[2]   This meant a big attendance on the army of merchants and agents with their conveyance.

Ships do not seem to have been much used; on June 7 the "Good Year" of Lynn is to carry fodder and other victuals to Scotland, and on June 14 the "Rose of Arewell" is freighted with wine for the same quarter.[3]   A few others are a month and more earlier.   On the other hand from twenty-one sheriffdoms a supply of waggons is ordered of two classes, the one drawn by four strong horses, the other by eight oxen; 106 of the former and 110 of the latter, which added to the number of animals to be provided

[1] *Vita Edw.* pp. 206-7; Baker of Swinbroke in *Chronicon Angliae*, ed. Giles, p. 55.

[2] *Rotuli Scotiae*, i. pp. 125-6.

[3] *Rotuli Scotiae*, i. pp. 127, 128.   Again we must distinguish the long list of ships freighted for the proposed campaign at Easter.   There is no indication that these had anything to do with the Bannockburn campaign, which apparently depended on its land transport.   *Rot. Scot.* i. pp. 114 ff.

for 424 horses and 880 oxen.[1] The four-horsed waggons (*quadrigae, carectae*) alone, if extended in a line, and these must here include others not expressly levied, would have stretched for twenty miles.[2] For not only food and drink, but armour, tents and furniture had thus to be brought along; according to Barbour eighty waggons were charged with "fuel," which would seem here to have the sense of "food" generally.[3] At any rate the amount of wheeled transport must have been enormous, and we may well ask how it would have fared on the rough, scanty highway over the moor at St. Abb's Head, which "must have been a mere bridle path and impassable for wheels,"[4] or how it could have negotiated the difficulties at the ravine of Cockburnspath.

Fortunately we are not left entirely to con-jecture, for on June 18 King Edward is credited with issuing a particular order to the Archbishop of Canterbury and his council from "Soltre."[5]

[1] *Rotuli Scotiae*, i. p. 127.
[2] *Vita Edw*. p. 202.
[3] See *New Eng. Dict.* under "Fuel."
[4] *Local History and Antiquities*, Morris and Jordan, p. 238.
[5] Bain, iii. No. 365.

This is Soutra, the parish in which rises Soutra Hill, the western bastion of the Lammermuirs, on which stood an hospital for travellers since the twelfth century, as on a direct and common route down Lauderdale from Edinburgh to the valley of the Tweed. The evidence is small but 'twill serve. A march from Dunbar would not have brought Edward and his army within miles of Soutra. The actual date may not signify much within a few days,[1] but the inference is plain. The English host came up the Tweed valley, whether starting as a whole from Berwick or in part from Wark *via* Coldstream, and took the road through Lauderdale. Thus we see why it is that Barbour, in describing their march, speaks of them as covering "hills and valleys," but says no word of the sea or of special difficulties on the track. Tweeddale and Lauderdale was the route and not the coast.

[1] The date on such documents does not imply presence in the place on that particular day. Here it is probably post-dated, for it would bring Edward to Edinburgh on the 19th, though Barbour says he did not leave, at least, before the 22nd. There is no suggestion that the army stayed anywhere more than a night, though it may have done so at Edinburgh to get in stores from the ships at Leith. But this is conjecture.

CHAPTER III.

DISPOSITIONS. THE FIRST PHASE:
SUNDAY, JUNE 23.

THERE is no fairer scene in Scotland than the
cockpit of battles long ago that lies round
Stirling. On guard the rock lifts its walled and
once a towered crest above the lowest fords,
where the Forth deeply curves and recurves
through the plain, glimmering here and there
from the level like a sword hidden in the grass.
And a sword it was to prove in its slaying on
the day when the ancient river, like Kishon and
Scamander, fought for the homeland. South of
the rock and its long eastern declivity intervenes
a saucer-shaped tract of ground, but longitudinal
rather than circular, roughly defined by outlying hills and bare or grassy cliffs, rising at
its highest to 200 feet, elsewhere varying from
100 to 50, and sinking to an inner valley, which

at its outmost reach dips to the Bannock Burn as it flows towards the Forth. Midway the valley is humped like a camel by Coxet Hill. The burn, passing the corner of the eastern rim that leads back by St. Ninians to Stirling, twists, with one great swoop northwards, through the flat expanse that bounds the river, a flat that gradually sinks until it is only the height of the bank above water.

But more accurately to reproduce the four-teenth century landscape, trim fields and en-closures must dissolve in rough rigs and meadow, and the straggling outskirts of the Torwood bristle over the undulations to the south; the river banks, and the banks of the Bannock as it draws to its exit, be fringed with great blobs or lagoons of water, prob-ably flooded at high tide, and soaking round in muddy patches and channels. So marked a feature of the ground were these lagoons that it was known as "the Pools"; and it was while struggling through these that the English bag-gage was picked up after Stirling Bridge by the Steward and Lennox who, like Rob Roy at

Sherrifmuir, stood by for booty.[1] Next cover the plateau and its inner hollow with an irregular natural growth of trees to give the New or King's Park of Alexander III., a game preserve for residents in the castle. Near by the eastern corner comes the " Roman " or mediaeval road, continued in an " entry " or passage way through the wood, probably similar to the "entry" of Jedburgh Forest in which Douglas trapped an English column three years later, wide at the mouth but narrowing like the flat-iron shape of shield to an inconsiderable width.[2] But the Forth and the Bannock, the pools and marshes and "sykes," or channels, of the Carse, and the trees, with the entry of the New Park, are the elements of the landscape that determine the operations to follow.

II.

King Robert mustered his men in the Tor-wood between Falkirk and the neighbourhood

---

[1] Hemingburgh, ii. p. 140. He calls the ground the " Polles." Bruce was watching this line, the "Polles," for Edward in March, 1304 (Stevenson, *Documents*, etc., ii. pp. 468, 470).

[2] *Bruce*, xvi. 310, etc.

of Stirling, a familiar centre for such gatherings. By the close of May it was known at English headquarters that the Scots were taking position in strong and marshy places on the Stirling road, where access was difficult for horsemen,[1] but no practical use was made of a knowledge which might have been anticipated. Bruce found his soldiers a likely lot to his experienced eye and in good spirits, a frame of mind which he encouraged by his personal welcome and attention to such as he came across,[2] a demo-cratic interest and ease developed by his enforced familiarity of years with the huts where poor men lie and the men and women therein. Here again there was a wide diversity in the attitude of mind characterising the leaders of either host, and, as a result, a difference in *morale* of fundamental value. The Scots were made to feel that every man was fighting his own battle.

And the king's plan of action, as he explained it to his staff, was simple enough. The English were coming to rescue the castle; it was their

---

[1] *Foedera*, iii. No. 481.   [2] *Bruce*, xi. 255-260.

cue to close the ways against them, or obstruct them as much as they could. The ways to the castle were two;[1] there was the one through the New Park, which it seems to have been thought they would prefer, and there was the other on the level past the marshes of the Forth. In the former case the horsemen, the core of the enemy's force, would be seriously hampered by the trees; in the latter the unsafe condition of the ground would be equally disconcerting. It was out of the question to attempt to match the English horse; it was therefore the Scottish cue to get them entangled in a difficult place, and oppose to them the mobility of men on foot in light armour, independent of such difficulties.

With this general idea the army was divided into four "battles." The vanguard was assigned to Randolph, Earl of Moray, with whom was the general mass of men of higher rank, while Bruce himself took the rear directly behind the earl; his force including his own Carrick following with contingents from Cantyre, Argyll, Bute

[1] For all this see *Bruce*, xi. 270 and following lines.

46

and the Isles and many Lowlanders. Between these came the other two divisions, parallel to each other but somewhat to the side of van and rear. On these lines it would fall to the king to act as a reserve for support to whatever division was hard pressed. But in this arrangement there was no fixity; circumstances were to alter the case. The command of one body was given to Edward Bruce, of the other to Walter the Steward, with whom, on account of his "beardless" youth, was associated James Douglas, and it is virtually Douglas who acts as leader. The Scottish captains had no room for personal jealousies.

On Saturday morning, the 22nd, King Robert's scouts reported that the English had spent the previous night at Edinburgh. Thereupon he retired to the position in the New Park. Still inclined to the opinion that the enemy would prefer the road in this direction he set about adding to its natural difficulties. His major fear, as at Loudoun Hill, was that of finding his men surrounded by a swarm of horsemen. Wallace had provided for this by a circular formation of the "schiltrom,"[1] but to make this effective required a good many in the ranks, or the power of the spear-armed column was dissipated. Bruce seems to have preferred the oblong formation, which gave at once greater backing and impetus. On the other hand the flanks were exposed.

It was to deal with this defect and narrow the fighting to the width of his own front that, at Loudoun Hill, he had dug three lines of trenches inwards from the outlying bogs towards the road. This enabled him to use to the fullest such strength as he could command, while he was ensured from interference on his flanks by the obstacles of the ditches. So here, in front of the entry, facing south to the Torwood, was "ane playne feld" or level space across which came "the way." Manoeuvring on such favourable ground was now made impossible by having it dug over into "pits" or "pottis," a foot across,[2] the depth of a man's

[1] A "schiltrom" was a "shield-troop" or a close-packed body of men walled by the shields.

[2] Much has been made of the assumed trapping of the horse in the pits. Barbour says no more of them for the

knee, and as thickly set as cells in a honey-
comb for a considerable distance out on either
side of the approach. Grass laid upon sticks
made of these impediments a trap whose extent

plain reason that, as will be seen, they never had a chance.
Nor are historians satisfied with Barbour's description of their
position ; geographical features have so altered (xi.) :

> 360 " in ane playne feld, by the way,
> " Quhar he thoucht neid behufit away
> " The Inglis men, gif that thay wald
> " Throw the Park to the castell hald.
>
>   .   .   .   .   .   .
>
> 387 " On athir syde the way weill braid
> " It wes pottit."

But according to Lord Hailes's interpretation they were dug
"in every quarter where cavalry could have access" (*Annals*,
ii. p. 50)—a big order indeed. Tytler puts them in "a field"
on Bruce's left at St. Ninians as an obstacle to any attack by the
garrison of the castle (*History*, i. 260)—surely a displacement.
Hill Burton precisely allots them to "a tract of flat ground
through which an army might pass to the gate of Stirling
Castle" (*History*, ii. 263)—that is on the Carse. Neither Tytler
nor Burton explains how Clifford's horsemen missed them, either
coming to St. Ninians or fleeing to the castle. Maxwell
describes as "honeycombed" "the ground between the two
bogs" (bogs of which no contemporary writer makes any
mention) "and also the hard ground opposite the right of his
lines" (*Robert the Bruce*, 202-3): and Mr. Lang agrees. In face
of such conclusions one does not venture lightly to differ ; only
an appeal to facts can justify it. Professor Hume Brown, ever
fair and sagacious, declares that "the conflicting authorities do
not enable us to decide" what was "the nature" of the "pots" or
"in what part of the field they were relatively placed" (*History*,
i. 159). Barbour, who chiefly mentions them, says they were in

could not be estimated because they were concealed. They could not be prepared for, because they would be discovered only in the experience of their mischief. The construction of these pitfalls was a night's work, and the king himself inspected them to his satisfaction next morning.

Rising was early, very soon after sunrise, which at this time of the year takes place a few minutes after 4 a.m. Mass inaugurated the day, which, as the vigil of St. John, brought no dinner and only bread and water for refreshment; fighting would have to be done on an empty or sodden stomach, a poor heartener in a desperate fray. But when all stood to arms, and the king made proclamation that any one who felt he had no heart in the business or qualms

front of Bruce's position at the entry, and describes them minutely with measurements. Friar Baston says that in the holes were stakes (*palis*). An early edition of Tytler contains a communication from a military friend asserting that the pits were still discernible in " Halbert Marsh " when it was being drained. Could pits be dug to make the bog unsafe? The later editions of Tytler do not contain this communication (cited in Burns's *War of Independence*, ii. 550). At Cressy (1346) the English dug many " pits," a foot wide and deep, to check possible pursuit by the French cavalry (Baker, p. 166).

of timidity should retire, and only men prepared for the last extremity remain, the general cry was that no fear of death would hinder them from a fight to a finish. Thereupon all the servants and "small folk" were sent with the baggage well into the Park, where they disposed themselves out of the way in a valley.[1]

The disposition of the troops, thereafter, was determined by the object of blocking the English line of advance, which of the two possible routes would be chosen being unknown. Randolph with the vanguard was therefore posted at the old kirk of St. Ninians

---

[1] *Bruce*, xi. 426. This is the only mention of the disposition of the servants, yet, despite the fact that Barbour expressly says they were sent to a valley, it has been generally believed and is always stated that they were on a hill, to wit "the Gillies' (*i.e.* Servants') Hill," a Gaelic name. It is probably a personal name applied to the hill. "The names both of Gillies and Morison occur in the muirlands" (*Old Stat. Acct.* xviii. p. 392). In this same quarter we have the legend of the "Borestone," which "from a hole in its centre is said to have supported Bruce's standard." Flags in the fourteenth century were for carrying not sticking in stones, and Bruce ordered his men to have plenty of them. And why a stone which could not keep a flag-pole and flag upright if there was the slightest wind, when there was the solid earth?

to check any attempt to pass by the level.[1]
Bruce, himself, with his division occupied the
entry to meet the possible attack there. Edward
Bruce and Douglas were to act as supports in
whichever quarter need arose; Edward obviously being nearer his brother, Douglas and
the Stewart in Randolph's neighbourhood.[2]
Such were the Scottish dispositions in the

[1] "Besyd the kirk (*i.e.* St. Ninians) to keep the way,"
etc., *Bruce*, xi. 442, etc. Nothing could be clearer than the
position of Randolph "with his menyhe," but writers have
been unfortunate in finding that this does not quite fit in with
the way they have realised the affair. "Randolph," says Sir
Herbert Maxwell, "was probably stationed on Coxet Hill"
(*Robert the Bruce*, p. 214 note). Professor Oman keeps him at
St. Ninians but gives him, with Bruce, "only small detach-
ments" (*History of the Art of War*, p. 573), though Barbour
gives each his full array. Keeping tightly to the Torwood disposition Mr. Lang sets Randolph "to lead the vaward and watch
against any attempt to throw cavalry into Stirling" (*History of
Scotland*, vol. i. p. 219). This is to anticipate: Randolph's task
was to block advance that way, as Bruce undertook to do at the
entry. Tytler puts him in command of "the vaward or centre"—
which is vague (*History*, ed. 1841, pp. 262-3), and Mr. Burns
rounds off by assigning to him "the command of the centre
division in the coming battle," with "a special commission," "a
temporary command" to watch the Carse (*The Scottish War
of Independence*, vol. ii. pp. 314, 252). Each assumes it to have
been but an incidental precaution, when it was really an integral
part of the dispositions.

[2] See pp. 58, 61.

New Park on Sunday morning. Their very simplicity and obviousness have been a snare to the historians.

III.

The English had reached Falkirk by Saturday evening and were now within ten miles of Stirling. Edward had tarried overlong at Berwick, and it had been a hurried march so far. On the Saturday the army had done more than twenty miles from Edinburgh, good marching in the hot, dry June weather of that year. But forcing the journey had proved exhausting to both men and horses. Little time could be spent in sleep, even less on food, so that horses, riders and footmen alike were weary and hungry.[1] Nevertheless in appearance and size the host was exceedingly formidable, and profoundly impressed the vedette of horsemen under Sir Robert Keith, the Marshal, and James Douglas, whom Bruce had sent forward to report. That might well be. It covered and stretched over a great space of ground; it reflected the sun's rays from thousands of spears

[1] *Vita Edw.* p. 202.

and shields and polished helmets; banners, standards and pennons hung thick above them over the bright surcoats and garish devices of the knights, the russet and green and grey of the infantry, the bright cloaks or khaki-like linen tunics of the Irish and Welsh, the spare horses, the various equipments, the huge baggage train and miscellany of servants; and in front of them, as frail opposition, only "few folk of ane sympill land."[1] The unfavourable account of the scouts was made to the king privately, and he, always heedful of the psychological element of *morale*, deliberately misreported what they had said, causing it to be told that the enemy was coming on in confusion and thereby raising the spirits of his deluded army.[2]

Edward had constituted his force in ten divisions,[3] of which the Earls of Gloucester and Hereford took the van with their horse and Welsh foot. Two or three miles out he was met by Sir Philip Mowbray from the castle, who must have ridden with a company round by the Carse. Mowbray's suggestion was that

[1] *Bruce*, xi. 202. [2] *Ibid.* 454-97. [3] *Ibid.* 155-6.

he should come no farther, since, as he put the understanding, the English had come within three miles of the castle within eight days of June 24, and he was therefore relieved.[1]   But they had not marched so far to take cover in a technicality ; they had come to destroy the Scots at one blow.   Further, Mowbray informed them that the Scots had blocked the narrow ways of the wood, intelligence which may indeed have altered the original purpose of entering by that road, as Bruce had thought likely.   Clearly it was Mowbray's idea that the Scots were not to be taken cheaply, and that the enterprise on hand was not so easy as it looked.   It was now "after dinner," about midday.

To this meeting may be attributed the episode which seems to have followed upon it.   Three hundred horsemen [2] under Sir Robert Clifford

---

[1] *Scalacronica*, p. 141.

[2] *Ibid.* p. 141.   Barbour makes them 800.   *Lanercost* says it was the English van (*prima acies*) which was led by Clifford, but in this there is a mistake, as the other accounts show. Apparently this was the first move, which would have given rise to the confusion.   But the van was not necessarily in the front of the fighting.   Bruce's rearguard and vaward were engaged almost simultaneously at the entry and at St. Ninians.

and Henry de Beaumont were dispatched to take the Carse road and enter the castle, so as to complete the relief, or, as another version puts it, to surround the wood and prevent the Scots getting away.[1] They eluded the notice of Randolph till they were below his position, wherefore Bruce bluntly told him that "ane rose of his chaplet was faldyn"; he had neglected his duty. Possibly by this time all Scottish eyes were concentrated on the first appearing of the enemy from the cover of the Torwood. Stung by the reproach, Randolph rushed his men down to the level, five hundred in number. It looked a rash proceeding, for it was confronting horse with foot,[2] and the horse might well have ridden on.

But no mediaeval knight would refuse so obvious a challenge.

"Let us retire a little," shouted Beaumont, "let them come on; give them room." A Yorkshire knight, Sir Thomas Gray, remarked

---

[1] *Lanercost*, p. 225.

[2] But White, in his *History of the Battle of Bannockburn*, will have it that Randolph had horse, following Buchanan, Godscroft and Holinshed!

that probably the Scots would soon take more than they got. This was the place for the usual feudal retort, " If you are afraid, you can go." " Not for fear," was the reply, and Gray, spurring on the Scots, had his horse pierced with the pikes, was brought to ground and taken prisoner.[1] Randolph had formed his men into a hollow schiltrom,[2] round which the impenetrable spears bristled like the spines of a hedgehog. Sir William Deyncourt rashly followed Gray, had a similar experience, and was killed.

The others acted more circumspectly. They surrounded the Scots, charging from every quarter without forcing an opening; their horses fell under the gashes of the spears, and their tumbled riders were slain. In their fury they took to throwing their weapons against their rock-like foes, till spears, darts and knives, swords and maces rose in a heap within the Scottish lines.[2] Of the Scots some even rushed

---

[1] *Scalacronica*, p. 141. Sir Thomas Gray was father of the author.

[2] So it would appear from Barbour's expression : "inwith thame ane montane was of wapnys" (xi. 601-2). Cf. next paragraph for the "montane."

from the ranks to bring down a man. Thus the fight clattered on, while the steam from striving men and horses, with the tossed-up dust from the plain, almost hid the combatants.

Douglas, seeing Randolph so hard pressed, asked leave to go to his help, which Bruce granted; but when he came near he saw signs of wavering among the assailants, and anxious to let the earl have all the credit he deserved, he stayed his men and advanced no farther. Indeed, Randolph was presently doing the pressing himself, and, pushing on, cut the English squadron in two, of which one part rode off to the castle and the other retired to the main body, both in utter disorder, while the Scots, having lost but one yeoman, took off their helmets to ease themselves of the heat and stuffiness.[1] Thus was consummated the

---

[1] Randolph's charge of foot upon horse is all-important as a precedent, as also the similar advance against the vanguard by Bruce. Barbour says of Randolph that when his opponents became shaky, "In hy apone them can he ga, And pressit thame" (xii. 132-3); in *Lanercost* it is he rushed upon Clifford's body of men—*irruerunt in eam* (p. 225).

defeat of a regiment of horse by a column of infantry, a thing unheard of.[1]

Meantime, for the events seem to have synchronised, though that involving the Earl of Moray was of longer duration, King Robert himself "at the other part of the wood"[2] was engaged in a not dissimilar fashion. The young bloods of England had repudiated the suggestions of Mowbray, and the advance guard in particular, under Gloucester and Hereford, pushed out of the Torwood to engage the Scots. As Henry de Bohun, Hereford's nephew, came out with his Welshmen upon the cleared ground, they could see the Scots moving about on the skirts of the wood in front. Bruce, indeed, was getting his men into their positions, anticipating an immediate attack. To the observation of the oncomers it seemed as if the Scots were already in flight.

---

[1] It is true that at Courtrai in 1302 Flemish foot had defeated French horsemen. Gray says the Scots had taken this as an example (*Scala.* p. 142). But Randolph's affair had special features.

[2] *Scala.* p. 141. The wood, then, extended from Bruce's position at the entry to St. Ninians slope.

Thus falsely emboldened de Bohun conceived the idea of himself either slaying the Bruce or bringing him off a captive to his king. But as they came to closer quarters the illusion passed; the Scots were found not to be on the run, and in greater numbers than could safely be tackled. De Bohun turned his horse as the signal for a retiral, to find that his proposed victim, King Robert himself, had ridden out from cover and was in his front.[1] The king was mounted on a pretty little grey pony, and above his conical steel cap or bassinet he wore a cap of hardened leather on which was attached a high crown, while in his hand he held only a battle-axe. It was a clear defiance, and no knight could have ignored it, all the more as, fully weaponed on a heavy steed, the chances were in de Bohun's favour. Driving on his horse he thundered, with lance in rest, towards the advancing king, missed him, and, as he lumbered past, Bruce smashed in his skull at a blow, breaking his own

[1] *Vita Edw.* p. 202. With this English account Barbour corresponds. Yet in Shearer's *Fact and Fiction in the Story of Bannockburn* (Stirling, 1909) the affair is dismissed as fiction. Gray, wrongly, calls the knight Peris de Mountforth.

axe-shaft, while his stricken opponent plumped to the ground.

It was summons for a Scottish advance. The English van, already partly in retreat, under such brilliant discouragement forbore to make a stand. De Bohun's squire, gallantly standing by his dead master, was overwhelmed; Gloucester was unhorsed, and his division thrust back with considerable slaughter. And just as Douglas had moved up to support the Earl of Moray, so here we find Edward Bruce preparing to do a similar service in his brother's case.[1]

The one anxious moment for the Scottish commanders in the neighbourhood had been the king's rash invitation to the English knight; it was a rare flash of that impetuosity so marked in his brother's case and exampled once before at Dumfries; it was risking too much, and they did not fail to let him know their judgment, to which he answered nothing, showing regret only for the breaking of his battle-axe. Presently there was another dis-

[1] *Bruce*, xii. 345.

traction, as the soldiers moved away to give a royal reception to Randolph on his return from a hard-fought and entirely successful engagement.

In effect Bruce had hit his foes one dolorous stroke, as Randolph had another. It shows how high yet stood the significance of personal conflicts, the fall of individual knights, and how narrow the edge of military confidence, that the loss of a few conspicuous leaders and the repulse of small bodies of horse should have acted upon the general mind on both sides in so powerful a fashion, elating the victors and in an even greater proportion depressing the beaten side, though their power remained substantially intact. Bruce fully realised the value of this result ; as he is made to say in the speech that followed :

> "fra the hert be discumfite,
> The body is nocht worth a myt."

Twice in one afternoon they had repulsed the attack of their foes. Foot had stood up to mailed horsemen and broken them, had even attacked and been successful. And they had done so without having to utilise any advantage of ground. The "pots" had not come into play, probably from the straggling nature of the English approach to the entry ; Randolph had fought upon the "playne feld." Things had even exceeded expectation. Yet Bruce was cautious, or professed to be so. Addressing his men he pointed out how well they had done, and forecasted that such a beginning was bound to have a good ending ; yet he preferred to leave with them the settlement of the question whether they should continue as they had begun or retire with their laurels ; thus again displaying that sense of comradeship in a common cause which was so great a part of his popular strength. He would lead but he would not drive. The answer was a unanimous demand to be brought to battle as soon as next morning dawned.[1]

It was probably later in the day that Sir Alexander Seton secretly left the English camp and made his way to that of Bruce, where, it is said, he found the purpose of retreating to the

[1] *Bruce*, xii. 170-206.

Lennox country behind still a likely move if not settled on by the Scots; a plan against which he protested, telling the king that now, if ever, was his time to win the country, for the English were in deep discouragement, that they were in mortal dread of a sudden, open attack, and pledged himself to be drawn, hanged, beheaded and quartered—the traitor's sentence —if by attacking them in the morning he did not win with little loss.[1]

However these things may have been, the main facts stand out clearly; the English were perilously dispirited, shaken in nerve and fearful [2]—their lords had to issue a reassuring message;[3] the Scots were highly pleased with themselves, and Bruce was finally committed to an assault at dawn upon an already cowed but still formidable enemy. Thus the occurrences

---

[1] *Scala.* p. 141.

[2] "From that hour great fear was set up among the English and greater boldness among the Scots" (*Lanercost*, p. 225). "The English had been put out of countenance and were exceedingly dispirited by what had occurred" (*avoint pardi countenance, et etoint de trop mal covyne pur la journée passé. Scala.* p. 143).

[3] *Bruce*, xii. 370-382.

64

of this first day are of crucial importance in their effect upon what the second day was to bring to fruition.   And through all the psychological factor takes a determining place.

CHAPTER IV.

BANNOCKBURN. THE SECOND PHASE: MONDAY, JUNE 24.

WEARY, puzzled and disheartened, as the afternoon was now declining to evening, and it had been determined there should be no more fighting that day, the English host streamed out from the way through the Torwood and prepared to take quarters for the night. It is absolutely vital to understand clearly where their place of lodgment was, and on that point we are, fortunately, left with no opening for doubt. "Thair thai herbryit thame that nycht Doune in the Kers," writes John Barbour, and the English Sir Thomas Gray, whose father was captured by Randolph's men, is even more explicit: leaving the Torwood, he says, "they came out on a plain fronting the Water of Forth, beyond Bannock Burn, a bad, deep,

66

streamy morass, where the said host of the English settled down."[1] That is, they have placed themselves within the roughly triangular ground between the burn and the river, among the "pools" (as Barbour notes), sykes or water-channels and mudflats lying along the banks; in front the slightly higher and drier level of the "playne-land,"[2] upon which had just occurred the engagement with Moray, and behind that the wooded bluffs of the plateau that were the eastern limit of the New Park.

On the right and falling to the rear was the Forth itself, on their left the channel of the Bannock, which they had to cross. This had proved an awkward passage. To negotiate the worst places, such as the pools, bridges had to be improvised, for which purpose material was taken in woodwork and thatch from houses near, while report ran among the Scots that men had come down from the castle itself bearing doors and windows (wooden shutters)

---

[1] *Bruce*, xii. 391-2 ; *Scalacronica*, p. 141-2.

[2] The "dryfield lands" of the *Old Statistical Account*, xviii. p. 388.

to ease the way for their friends.[1] All this had
to be done, moreover, out of reach of the Scots,
to whom a flank attack on a disordered enemy
taking up a position in such a place might well
be supposed to be tempting.

When the host had all got over on to a
divided recess of land three miles by two at
most in length and breadth, including what
was then marsh, and probably with not much
less than a mile of the length to be deducted
as giving a margin between themselves and
the enemy, we can well believe they were
cramped for room. It may further be in-
ferred that the English right lay opposite
Cambuskenneth, for that same night the Earl
of Atholl crossed and seized Bruce's supplies

[1] This bridging of bad places on the Bannock, with subsequent
losses at these in the retreat, combined with what he knew of
the pits from Baston's poem, which he cites, explains the
curious confusion set up in the mind of Baker of Swinbroke.
He says the Scots dug, in front of their position, long ditches
from right to left, covering them with frail structures of wicker-
work or "hordelles," *i.e.* "hurdles"—wicker doors were not
unknown in Scotland at a much later date—with turf and grass
above. At the first charge he tumbles the English horse into
this trench (*fossa*. Baker of Swinbroke, *Chronicle* (Ed. Giles),
pp. 56, 57. Also in *Chronicles*, Edw. I. and II. ii. p. 300). This
is just in Baker's combining way. Cf. note on p. 85.

there, killing Sir William of Herth (Airth) and many of his men.[1] No explanation of this curious fact has ever been offered in the accepted accounts.

Thus so far as the mere relief of the castle, in a technical sense, was concerned, the thing had been done; garrison and army were in touch. But that was now a small matter. The bigger issue was to be fought out, and, while the first moves had been wholly in the Scottish favour, the English army had placed itself in a position from which it could be safely extricated only by a swift and decisive victory.

It faced the enemy nearly parallel to its own line of advance, so that retiral was possible only by one flank and then over a serious obstacle; to the other flank and the rear was a dangerous river, with hostile country beyond. The ground was too restricted to allow of any freedom of movement, and round the lines it was soft and treacherous. Edward was trapped in the river bend as Simon de Montfort had been by his father at Evesham, and even in worse case.

[1] *Bruce*, xiii. 491-96.

Defeat would bring inevitable and horrible disaster. Determination in such circumstances not to take the offensive, but await attack, was the culmination of military folly.[1]

With all this in view, Bruce did not miss the significance of the English congested and fenced-in position. His tactical cue clearly was to carry out his purpose of attacking, to pin the enemy to their ground, cork the bottle in which they had inserted themselves, put a bar across between Forth and Bannock, contain their fighting front to his own span, and press and frighten the elbowing mass back through the death-gates in their rear. " Press, press," is the note of Bruce's general orders.[2] It was a brilliant conception in its utilisation of the characteristics of the ground, as it was daring in advancing foot to force the combat upon horse. But after all the obviousness of it was only to eyes that could see ; a cautious and routine mind would have seen some other course to be demanded, or refused so momentous a risk. Missing the point that, from this stage, the Scots were to

[1] *Vita Edw.* p. 203.   [2] Cf. pp. 58 (n.), 80 (n.).

take the aggressive, writers have misconceived everything.

II.

The English passed a bad night, in constant fear of a Scottish attack; there was no rest or sleep, the men remained under arms and the horses ready bitted. By morning it was ascertained that the Scots were ready for battle.[1] In the circumstances some of Edward's veteran knights and sage councillors advised postponement, alike in view of the solemnity of a saint's day and the exhaustion of the army. Once more, however, the young men had their way, scouting such advice as slothful and stupid.[2] This was more to the king's mind; he took no care about securing the patronage of saints, a point about which his father had always been particular, and he was fulfilled with confidence in his superior force. At Gloucester's suggestion of delay for the same reason, he blazed out in accusations of lying and treachery. "To-day," was the reply, "it will be clear that I am

[1] *Vita Edw.* 203; *Scala.* 142.   [2] *Vita Edw.* 203.

neither traitor nor liar," and the fated young earl passed to his doom.

More calmly the day of the Scots had opened with attendance at mass, after which there was a "sup" of bread and wine, and the knighting of men qualified for this honour on the field, Walter Stewart and James Douglas among the number, while Bruce issued his final orders with exhortations of encouragement. All this over, the Scots marched out boldly from the wood upon the plain on foot, while the English at sight of them hurried to climb into their saddles.[1] They were in four divisions,[2] thick with banners if they had adopted King Robert's suggestion, while the great mass of the opposing host, in a glitter as of a "heavenly" company [3] and much bannered too, showed no intervals between its

[1] *Scala.* 142.

[2] *Lanercost* says there were only three ; that two of these went in front of the third, one on the flank of the other, but neither of the two directly in front of the other—that is, they advanced in echelon—while the third followed under King Robert (p. 225). Except that a brigade is missing, this is roughly what occurred.

[3] Friar Baston in *Scotichronicon* : *Anglicolae quasi Coelicolae*, etc.

nine brigades, the straitened character of the ground compressing them all into one vast "schiltrom," with the van, the tenth brigade, alone standing out from the rest.[1]

Edward was amazed at the boldness of the Scottish advance; "What! will yon Scots fight?" he ejaculated. "Yea, truly," answered Sir Ingram de Umfraville, the Anglo-Scot, adding his tribute of wonder to see Scotsmen offering battle to the great might of England on a plain, hard field, and suggesting that it might be wise to withdraw behind their tents, when the opportunities of rich plunder would prove too alluring to their foes and they could attack them in confusion while so pleasantly employed. Bruce, indeed, had expressly warned his men against giving thought or eye to the riches in the English camp, which he nevertheless had dangled before their minds as an incentive, until such time as they had made victory good and sure.[2] However, Umfraville's

---

[1] *Bruce*, xii. 428-437 ; *Scala*. p. 142, "the battalions of the English were packed close" (*lez bataillis dez Engles qi entassez estoint*).

[2] *Bruce*, xii. 449, 475.

project was not to be tried ; the king would not withdraw before such a rabble.

At this stage the Scots were seen to halt and kneel in a moment of prayer. "They kneel to ask mercy," excitedly observed the king. "Not of you," said Sir Ingram ; "yon men will win all or die." "So be it," was the royal answer, and the trumpets sounded the call to action.[1]

The Scots had resumed their advance, the divisions taking a formation in echelon from the right, each to the flank of and rather behind that in front.[2] They were in closely packed

---

[1] *Bruce*, xii. 476-9 ; *Lanercost*, 225 : "Said a 'Pater Noster,' recommended themselves to God and asked the aid of heaven."

[2] See extract from *Lanercost* above. Though persistently ignored, the fact that the Scots moved against the enemy and forced the attack is absolutely clear from the accounts. Of course when the Scots moved the English responded, but it was the Scots first. Barbour's narrative rests on this. After the prayer, says the *Lanercost* chronicle, they (the Scots) "advanced boldly against the English" (*audacter contra Anglicos processerunt*, p. 225). "The aforesaid Scots came on in line of schiltroms and engaged the English battalions" (*Lez avaunt ditz Escotez vindrent de tot aleyn en schiltrome, assemblerent sur lez bataillis dez Engles*, p. 142). According to the *Vita Edwardi* writer, the Scottish leading schiltrom (*turma*) fiercely attacked the division under Gloucester (*aciem comitis G. acriter invasit*, p. 203). There is absolutely no shadow of a suggestion that the Scots simply took up a position and waited for attack ;

columns bristling with long pikes. The English van on the move thus encountered the leading column on the Scottish right under Edward Bruce.[1] Report had it that Gloucester and Hereford fell into dispute as to which should have the honour to lead off, Hereford urging that it pertained to him as Constable of England, Gloucester protesting that it was his right of custom since his ancestors had always held first place in the line of attack.[2] Without further parley he dashed upon the Scots, his horse was at once brought down, and he, having no support, was overwhelmed and slain ; much to the

that Bannockburn was a kind of Waterloo ; yet it is with this idea that most appear to work. Nor is there any mention of bogs anywhere, yet bogs have been imposed as defences of the Scottish front on the assumption that it kept its ground. Baker is the first to give a tactically passive rôle to the Scots, but the other four are dead against him. The rest—like making the rising sun shine on the faces of the English, with the remark that if they had waited till midday they would have had it on their right, both which are impossible any way, and that they were in three lines (horse, foot and religious)—he appears to owe to his imagination, like the modern accounts with which we are familiar.

[1] *Vita Edw.* errs in saying it was commanded by Douglas (p. 203).

[2] *Vita Edw.* p. 204. Gloucester had brought five hundred men at his own expense (*ibid.*).

75

later regret of the Scots, to whom as a prisoner held to ransom he would have proved more profitable, but having failed to don his emblazoned surcoat, he was unknown and perished in anonymity.[1] Of his five hundred personal followers, not one came to his aid ; they stood at gaze.

Presently they were busily occupied. The columns clashed together ; there was the preliminary smashing of spears, and rearing and rushing round and falling of deeply stabbed horses, and then a noisy medley of axe and spear music, as they struck upon iron helmet and harness. A rider brought to the ground would, like Gloucester, be unable, through weight of his armour, to rise unaided, and there was little pause for him to be saved from the death-stroke or suffocation.

Moray had by now brought up his division on Edward Bruce's left and, without hesitation, flung himself on the main mass of the English to the same accompaniment of breaking spears, "stickit" horses, and helpless, fallen men. The

[1] *Baker*, p. 57.

76

little body of Scots pressed home their assault, winning more and more room and cutting their way inwards, till they seemed lost among so many as if they had plunged into a sea.[1] At their heels came Douglas and the Steward, taking up the argument, "beside the Earl, a little by," but whether on right or left flank cannot be precisely stated. Some things suggest that Douglas entered between Edward Bruce and Moray, others that he was on the outer side of the latter ; it is not a matter of the first importance. Side by side the three "battles" of the Scots were now engaged, pressing with an irresistible vigour, but with "neither noise nor cry"; nothing to be heard beyond the groans of the wounded and blows as loud and remorseless as those of the Cyclops' hammers on the armour of Mars.

But here a serious interlude. According to one account, the battle had opened with an interchange of archery between the opposing forces, in which the English longbow showed its native

[1] "As thai war plungit in the se." How such a statement with its context is to be reconciled with the waiting for and acceptance of attack would pass the wit of man.

superiority.[1] Now the English archers were in
action again. There had been no tactical provision for their proper use, an oversight which was
not repeated in the actions of later years ; so that
here they seem to have drawn off and massed
themselves on the English extreme right flank,
whence they had the Scots on the unprotected
side.[2] Apparently, too, they faced inwards at
right angles or thereabouts to the English
fighting line.[3] This would be in accord with
their later dispositions.

But King Robert, who seems to have thought
of everything, had made provision for this peril.
His only mounted contingent, of five hundred
light horsemen under Sir Robert Keith, the
Marshal, suddenly charged the archers "at a
side," and had no difficulty in dispersing men
unprepared and unequipped to withstand such

[1] *Lanercost*, p. 226.

[2] Boece and Major say they were on the wings, but this is sheer
anachronism. That was a later combination, as at Dupplin
Moor and Halidon Hill, a lesson from Bannockburn. Baker
says that the wing position was of his day.

[3] Baker says they were in the rear, and had to shoot upwards,
for in shooting straight they hit mostly their own friends in the
back and but few Scots on the breast (*Chron.* 57-8).

an attack. Thus the archers were sorely cut up and definitely put out of action, some sheering off altogether, others rushing back upon their friends, who also swept them from their way in eagerness to get forward. On these now the Scottish archers, no longer outranged, played with effect, and, for once in their history, had the field to themselves.[1] Bruce saw how well the day was going, how hard and successfully his men were pressing, in what difficulties were his foes, how more pressure of the same sort and spirit was likely to force victory, and therefore flung his own reserve division into the fight, presumably occupying the ground from which the archers had been cleared and where the men from behind were making a stand.

Thus the line was closed and the whole of the Scottish army engaged on the English front, con-

---

[1] A contemporary story illustrates the activity of the Scottish archers. A Gascon knight, devoted to St. Francis, when the battle was at its height and the Scottish archers were going strong, called on the saint, who appeared in the habit of his order, and personally diverted the arrows. The knight's horse was horribly wounded by the Scottish pikes, which indicates their method of dealing with the mounted men (cited in Bryce's *Grey Friars*, vol. i. p. 23).

taining it and even pressing onwards.[1]   Directing their spears on the horses, they sorely dis-
abled them, and then had the riders much at
their will.   Blood dyed the grass to tragic red, and
scarves and blazonry steeped in its pools ; spears
were breaking under thrust and twist, weapons
clanging upon armour ; there was shouting of
war-cries on either side as men fell who in that
deadly press could never rise again.   Edward
Bruce had driven back the vanguard upon the
main body ;[2] Douglas and the Steward rushed
every opening ; Moray's men were diving ever
deeper ; there was a raging combat on the

---

[1] As already pointed out " pressing " was the Scottish note
of action ; Bruce is made to say :

> Quharfor I yhow requeir and pray,
> That, with all mycht that evir yhe may,
> Yhe press yhow at the begynnyng,
> But cowardis or abaysing,
> To meit thame that first sall assemmyll
> So stoutly that the henmast trymmyll.
> *Bruce*, xii. 263-8.

.   .   .   .

> That, be thai presit, I undirta,
> A littill fastar, yhe sall se
> That thai discumfit soyn sall be.
> xiii. 128-30.

[2] *Bruce*, xiii. 171-2.   " The Earl's command was smashed to
pieces " (*aciem comitis contritam, V.E.* p. 205).

king's flank; and all the time the Scots archers were grievously worrying men and killing horses.

On the Scottish side the cry passed along, "On them! on them! on them! they fail!" The English were jammed into helplessness; their numbers had become their snare. There was no clearing their front; their horses were piked and brought down, as a main feature of the fighting, or shook off their riders and rushed away; every movement backwards simply brought the Scots farther in. The rear could not get forward to supply fresh men: more than two hundred knights fled the field that day who had never drawn sword or struck a blow,[1] because they had never a chance. There was no getting round; on the one side was the Forth, on the other the Bannock, and the pools beside; in front was the moving wall of unbreakable Scots. Many noble men had fallen; no succour could be given; it seemed as if those behind must stand until the Scots had hewed a way to them over the bodies of their friends, when they

[1] *Vita Edw.* p. 205.

too would meet a similar fate.[1] And so discouragement and helplessness grew into uneasiness, and presently flamed out in nerveless panic.

It would be interesting could we say that Bruce had planned the amusing diversion which completed the discomfiture, but there is no hint in that direction. Probably it began in a growing emotion of curiosity. The baggage-keepers and servants secluded in the valley could not see, while hearing, what was going on; so, selecting a captain, they tied sheets on poles and spears to serve as banners, and under these menial ensigns two-thirds of them, apparently all the men, started forth to view the fight and give their lords such help as they could. This extraordinary intervention is well in keeping with the other unusual features of a paradoxical battle. Advancing in military order the camp-followers came within sight of the field, and, while yet a good distance away, raised the cry, "Slay! Slay! Upon them hastily."

---

[1] *Lanercost*, 225-6; *Scala*. 142. *Scalacronica* emphasises the Scottish spearing of the horses as driving the knights to fly.

THE BREAK-UP

To the English it seemed that fresh troops, equal in number to those already engaged, had arrived to join the Scots, and the shrinking in their lines became more evident. One more great heave on the part of the Scots, stronger pressure on the relaxing ranks, and the break-up began ; first in small companies here and there, leaving the proudest and bravest to keep it up a little longer, then King Edward himself and staff, and at the sight of the royal banner in flight the whole great army in riotous confusion.[1] A little longer and Edward might have been a captive, for adventurous Scots were already plucking at his charger's housings, and he had to clear himself with his mace.[2] In truth he was reluctant, but Valence, Earl of Pembroke, and Sir Giles de Argentine, personally responsible for his safety, forced him away ; the latter having done so turning again to meet his death with the remark, "I have never been accustomed to fly."[3]

[1] *Bruce*, xiii. 270-293 ; *Vita Edw.* 205.
[2] *Scala.* 142.
[3] "And lyis in Sanct Cuthbertis Kirk, beside Edinburgh " (Bellenden's *Boece*, Ed. 1821, ii. p. 393) ; *Scala.* 142.

The first resort of the royal party was the castle, which they found wisely barred to them. Why enter there? As the governor reminded them—and he had been in armour in the English ranks during the day—the castle would have to be surrendered, and with it then the king![1] As Mowbray afterwards attached himself to Bruce this action was put down as treachery, but no fair mind could give it such a meaning. With the help of a Scottish knight as guide[2] Edward's company was taken round the western side of the New Park, under cover of wood and cliff, and so off to the Lothians, hard pressed, as soon as their departure was discovered, by a handful of horsemen under Douglas, not enough to warrant attack though they kept the fugitives on the run. So they reached Dunbar, Despenser and Beaumont with the king, where a small boat was found to bring the choicest of the party to Berwick.

" The foe is chasit, the battell is done ceiss." Pitiable was the confusion that followed the general flight. Forced to the rear, many tried

[1] *Vita Edw.* 205 ; *Scala.* 142.   [2] *Lanercost*, p. 227.

to cross the Forth, of whom the most were drowned.[1] On the left was the passage over the Bannock Burn, where the improvised bridging was still in position among the pools, but this proved equally disastrous. In the crush of that terrified mob horses and men went down among the slime, few to rise again, so that those in front lay "for pavement to the abject rear, o'er-run and trampled on," and over a bridge of stifled dead one might pass dry-shod.[2]

---

[1] *Bruce*, xiii. 334-6 ; *Lanercost*, 227 : "Forth engulfed many well furnished with arms and coursers."

[2] *Bruce*, xiii. 337-40. "They fell back upon the ditch (*fosse*) of Bannockburn, each one tumbling upon the other" (*chescun cheoit sur autre. Scala.* p. 142). *Lanercost* speaks of it as a great pit (*magnam foveam*) into which riders fell with their horses, some getting out with difficulty, many others failing to do so. For this reason, he says, Bannockburn was on English lips for many a day to come. He explains that the tide enters the channel, another illuminating fact on the English position, which thus must have been near the mouth (p. 226). Mr. Lang has reproduced the reference in the words, "The Lanercost chronicler speaks of the sea-tide rushing up the Bannock burn and drowning the English" (*History*, i. p. 240). Mr. Lang has been, unwittingly, scarcely fair to the old chronicler. The *V.E.* author also speaks of a certain ditch (*fossa*) which swallowed up many (p. 205), which is therefore the Bannock channel, "betuix the brais," as Barbour puts it. The use for it of the term *fovea*, "a pit," as by the *Lanercost* writer, will explain how it came to be confounded with the artificial pits, as apparently by Fordun and

Meantime those held up by such obstacles and misadventures found themselves at the mercy of the Scots, and fell to the weapons of the camp rabble, who were busy carrying out their own earlier injunction of slaying.[1] Knights stripped off portions of their armour or all of it they could in order to run light. So fled Valence and Sir Maurice de Berkeley with a crowd of Welshmen conspicuous in their linen garments, of whom many were cut off.[2] These probably had got over the upper reach of the Bannock, avoiding the death-bridge nearer its mouth. For fifty miles the chase lasted, assisted, too, by loyalist Scots who had been English till this crushing blow broke their allegiance of fear.

A mass of foot, from the right and centre, took refuge on the castle crags, for the castle "was near," says Barbour, forcing King Robert to keep his men on hand lest they should make

by Baker; Fordun also saying that "many were drowned in the waters," *i.e.* the Forth (*Chronica Gentis Scotorum.* Skene, i. p. 347).

[1] *Bruce*, xiii. 341-5.

[2] *Annales Londonienses* in *Chronicles*, etc. i. p. 230; *Lanercost*, p. 228; *Bruce*, xiii. 417-26.

some desperate attempt against him, which check alone gave the English king his chance of escape, and was the saving of many others.[1] A further distraction was the colossal plunder of the English camp, its rich cloths, its gilt and silver vessels, and all the luxurious equipment of the noble campaigners, estimated in money value at £200,000,[2] or in modern proportion between two and three million pounds. Beyond this was a prospect of heavy ransoms, for the king's instructions had been rather to take captive than kill men of importance; a living knight had his cash value, a dead one none.

A big haul came from Bothwell Castle on the Clyde. Hereford, Sir Ingram de Umfraville, a crowd of knights, six hundred mounted men and one thousand foot set off by the western route down Clydesdale and Annandale for Carlisle. Arriving at Bothwell Castle, they were admitted into one of the few places still held for England, but the chief men only; the others were left to the attentions of the Scots, who were close at their heels. Of these abandoned ones two-thirds were slain, and others captured, many knights even falling to the countrywomen. Those who had been received as guests fared no better; Sir Walter Gilbertson, the treacherous governor, made his peace with King Robert by immediately putting them in custody and then delivering them to Edward Bruce, whom the king had dispatched thither. All others and those who surrendered on the rock ultimately found their way to Berwick.[1]

Of the figures of the Bannockburn dead there can be no counting; besides those on the field there must have been at least as many who met their fate on the countryside, following one or other of the great highways or going at large. Of the squires and the foot it is said the most part was not slain.[2] In the circumstances

---

[1] *Bruce*, xiii. 401-16; *Illustrations*, etc. (Stevenson), p. 2; *Lanercost*, 228; *Ann. Lond.* p. 231. Gilbertson is ancestor of the House of Hamilton.

[2] *Ann. Lond.* p. 231. Here there is a list of thirty-seven knights slain at "the battle of Stirling." Baker says about 300 men-at-arms were among the slain (p. 57). Bower gives 200 knights besides Gloucester (*Scotichron.* ii. p. 250). Walsingham from his MS. source fixes the number of knights and squires who fell at 700 (*Hist. Anglicana*, p. 141). See further note in my edition of the *Bruce*, p. 445.

we might expect the loss to fall heaviest on the knights and mounted men generally, so far as the actual field was concerned; except the archers the foot never really came into action. The estimates of slain horsemen vary from 154 to 700, and between 200 and 700 in the two MSS. of the *Bruce*. A later source gives 300 men-at-arms as the loss in this category. Even the highest figure does not go very high, but in mediaeval battles individual losses among the heavy cavalry had an importance beyond the mere numbers; Gloucester did not count for merely one. Far more than in Napoleon's day could it be said, as he put it: "Success in battle depends not so much on the number of men killed as upon the number frightened."

To the dead Bruce gave honourable burial according to rank. Earl Gilbert of Gloucester was matter of regret; he was a relative of the king. When the latter went out to inspect the field the day after, he was approached by a knight who had hid his armour in a bush; it was Sir Marmaduke de Twenge, the hero of Stirling Bridge, who was watching for a chance

M   89

of honourable surrender. Sir Marmaduke was handsomely treated and sent home without any exaction of ransom.[1] The ransomed personages run to more than 500. For the recovery of her husband by exchange Hereford's wife received all the Scottish captives retained since the time of Edward I., numbering over fifteen and including Bruce's wife, daughter and sister, with the venerable and now blind patriot, Robert Wishart, Bishop of Glasgow.[2] On the whole Bruce acted in so becoming and handsome a manner over these transactions that one English chronicler reports how " the hearts of many who were opposed to him he turned, in a wonderful way, to feeling an affection for him."[3] Always on the humane side Bruce is conspicuous.

What need to point any moral? Never did the arms of England suffer so complete a disaster; never did the arms of Scotland repeat so remarkable a performance. But it was the vanquished who learned the military lesson,

[1] *Bruce*, xiii. 515-37.   [2] *Vita Edw.* pp. 206, 208.
[3] *Annales Trokelowe*, p. 87.

and on the fields of France they showed, in the use of foot and archers in preference to the charging column of knights, how deep that lesson had been driven. Poictiers and Agincourt were won under the rock of Stirling.[1]

For the Scots it proved a disastrous precedent. Not by forgetting Bannockburn, but by putting its forward tactics into mechanical operation in circumstances wholly altered, did they invite the defeats of Dupplin Moor and Halidon Hill. Falkirk, and Courtrai—where the flower of the French chivalry was, in 1302, broken on the pikes of the Flemish burghers—and Bannockburn mark the downfall of the mediaeval trust in the armoured and mounted knight, and open the way to changes in the art of war, which, by raising the importance of a hitherto despised class, was not without important results, as Froissart notes for Courtrai, upon social and political history.

Meantime, for Scotland, Bannockburn was a cardinal event; off and on, for twenty more years, the struggle for independence was to be

[1] Baker, p. 252.

prolonged, but never again with as deep doubtings as before that encounter; in the darkest hour the memory of the great victory would flash over a stormy sea its message of the possibility and promise of success.

Note.—In a crude illustration in the Corpus Christi (Cambridge) MS. of the *Scotichronicon* the Scots at Bannockburn are shown on the Carse with Stirling Castle and town to their left and the Bannock Burn, therefore, to their right. The English are before them, also beyond the line of the Bannock. This is the position expounded above. The MS. is of the fifteenth century (Skene). See *National MSS. of Scotland*, vol. i. part ii. p. 69.

CHAPTER V.

BANNOCKBURN IN LATER HISTORY.

SOMETHING remains to be said of the confusion, as I contend, into which different historians have brought the details of the battle. A puzzled handling of some of these under pressure of a misconception has been indicated in the notes; but it is well to remember that these careful studies have also helped to enlightenment. Still it is unfortunate that in their inability to reconcile their statements with the facts of the sources, critics are apt to turn upon these and disparage them. Professor Hume Brown is perhaps the frankest: "these authorities themselves are both brief and obscure, and, in general, entitled to no implicit faith."[1] If this is accepted, then the foregoing chapters have been written in vain. I trust not. "Brief"

[1] *History*, i. p. 158, note.

93

is a relative term; Barbour gives the battle a pretty fair share in the greater part of three whole books, and, though we might all wish more, the other writers of that century, on the English side, are fairly generous—generous enough to leave the main lines clear. Differences in some minor details might be expected, indeed absolute similarity would arouse suspicion; but, if I have written aright, the general obscurity is due not to these writers but to their interpreters. If the former speak of one thing and the latter persist in asking for another, of course there is bound to be a complaint of "obscurity," of "conflict and confusion."

The truth is that a good many seem to have settled in their minds that Bannockburn was fought in a particular place in a particular way, and must have it so at all costs. It appears to them as a sort of Waterloo. Without enlarging upon their individual differences, it may be said for them that they conceive Bruce's task to have been to stop the English from reaching Stirling Castle; they therefore plant his forces in a line across the south end of the New Park

with the Bannockburn in front and the English
beyond, both forces thus extending east and
west and facing north (English) and south
(Scots). The English then make successive
charges upon the Scots in position. To get the
"cramping" and make defeat plausible, two
bogs are resuscitated in front of the Scottish position, features of which neither Scots nor English
chroniclers, who are usually pretty interested
in Scottish bogs, give the slightest hint; till,
what between pitting the whole Scottish front
"to the very flanks of the army," as Professor
Oman has it,[1] or "the ground between the two
bogs, and also the hard land opposite the right
of his line,"[2] with Sir Herbert Maxwell, one is
puzzled to see how the English horse ever got
near the Scots at all.

Moreover, the question would occur to any
one : if things were so, was there not a way
round ? It does occur to Sir Herbert Maxwell,
who responds that, beyond the mile of front he
has chosen, one way or the other, the banks of

[1] *History of the Art of War*, p. 572, note.
[2] *Robert the Bruce*, pp. 202-3.

95

the burn "are precipitous and impassable by cavalry."[1]   Then how did Clifford get his large body of mounted men across and cannily too? Where three hundred could go so easily, three thousand could, as Barbour and Gray say they did.   The same query presented itself to the mind of Sir Archibald Geikie, writing as a geographer, and he decides: "Across the impassable bogs and sheets of water of the Carse, the huge army of Edward could not march."[2]   It is only another example of the difficulties of interpretation which beset us that Sir Archibald, before coming to this decision, has just quoted the lines of Barbour which state that the English did actually pass on to the Carse by bridging the pools.

With the erroneous representation of the main battle goes a casual treatment of the two all-important engagements of the day before. The advance of the English van to the entry is reduced by Professor Hume Brown to a duel between Bruce and De Bohun "under circum-

[1] *Robert the Bruce*, p. 201.
[2] *Scenery of Scotland*, p. 403.

stances which are variously described."[1]   Reference to what I have said on this affair will show
facts that are thus overlooked ; it is an English
chronicler of the reign who tells that in it the
Earl of Gloucester, a commander of the English
van, was unhorsed.[2]   The same minimising of
the episode appears with writers in general,
and so a most significant repulse of an English
column degenerates to a personal affair of arms.
If the matter is thought worthy of acceptance, it
should surely be taken as a whole.   The "various
descriptions" are simply the Scottish and
English points of view ; the essential is that
there was a general engagement in which
"many (English) while following up the Scots
are slain."[3]

II.

As against all this I offer the account set out
in the preceding pages, based upon four authorities of the same century, of which the *Vita
Edwardi Secundi* is not later than *c.* 1325 ; the
author of the *Lanercost Chronicle* (*c.* 1346) says

---

[1] *History*, p. 158.   [2] *Vita Edw.* 202.
[3] *Vita Edw.* 202.

he has had his information from a trustworthy
person who was present; the *Scalacronica* is
the work of an English soldier whose father
was captured by Randolph's men, and who,
writing while a prisoner in Edinburgh Castle
(1355-7), confesses to have used chronicles of
the battle in the library there; and *The Bruce*
is of 1376, embodying, we may fairly infer, both
personal accounts and matter such as Gray
used. And, once we grasp the key, these
accounts fit into each other, and, obviously, each
from its own point of view tells the same story.
Which is this.

On Monday the eager English host dis-
charged two attacks on the Scots, one, which
Randolph destroyed, by the Carse road, and
one at the entry to the Park, which was repulsed
by Bruce's brigade. Bruce had expressly prepared for such, and so far was confining himself
to the defensive. That night the English
crossed into the Carse, as described in its place,
and there, next morning, were attacked by the
Scots, now taking the offensive. In a sense
there had been a change of front and plan,

consequent on the foolish move and the dis-
heartening of the English by their two previous
repulses. The "pots" and the Park, and all
the rest, were now at the back of the Scots,
as the Forth was at the back of the English,
who were outmanoeuvred and outfought. *Voilà
tout*.

And here let me say that, though I had
independently come to my conclusions from a
careful study of all the evidence, and though
his account is in other respects seriously defec-
tive, I am glad to find myself, at one important
stage, in agreement with Lord Hailes. He,
following Barbour, "after having examined the
ground," lays out the Scottish front "pretty
nearly upon the line of the present turnpike
road from Stirling towards Kilsyth";[1] that is,
as I do, at right angles to the commonly
accepted position, which he expressly refuses.
But Hailes allots this to both days, when
Barbour should have kept him right; the first
day's position was in the Park, the second day's
action on the Carse.

[1] *Annals* (1797), ii. p. 49, note.

III.

I now reduce the gist of the matter, in order to get the issues absolutely clear, to a set of three propositions for which I have already supplied the proofs in their place. They are as follows :

I. *The English army on Sunday evening crossed the Bannock and camped on the Carse.* This Barbour sets out, with explanation of how it was done; the *Scalacronica* distinctly says they passed on to "a plain before (*devers*) the water of Forth, over Bannockburn (*outre Bannokburn*), etc.," and the *Vita Edw.* allows us to infer the same.[1]

Now the whole case can be rested upon this fact, for the battle was fought on the ground between the encampments ; on that every one is substantially in agreement ; and there is neither record nor possibility of the English leaving the plain between the Bannock and Forth, to advance a mile or move up stream and fight below Brock's Brae, having first recrossed the

[1] Cf. chap. iv.

100

Bannock, which Maxwell, otherwise fully accept-
ing Gray's account, has said it was impossible
for heavy cavalry to do. He puts the passage
thus, "It was decided, apparently unwisely, to
bivouack in the carse near the river";[1] which
is scarcely sufficient.

Mr. Lang, who virtually accepts Sir Herbert's
account, strikes on the phrase "outre Bannockburn," and, being honestly mystified, gets
round it thus: Gray "must mean *south* of
Bannockburn, taking the point of view of his
father, at that hour a captive in Bruce's camp."[2]
But "that hour" didn't last for forty years;
and Barbour, who corroborates Gray, had no
geographical twist in his mind. Gray meant just
what he said, "beyond or over Bannockburn"
from the English side, that is north of the burn.
All assumptions that the battle was fought with
the burn between the armies thus go to wreck,
yet that is what we are asked to believe.

Less analytical, Mr. Robert White finding,
like the rest, that the facts do not fit his scheme,
decides, regretfully, that this is a "slip" on

[1] *Robert the Bruce*, p. 204.   [2] *History*, i. p. 221.

Barbour's part and avoids Gray.[1] The ground
the English camped on, he thinks, was only
a sort of a carse. But there is a lot still
unaccounted for, even if all these contentions
were successful. They plainly proceed from
an unwillingness to recognise the fact that
the English army was really in touch with the
castle; Mowbray had ridden down to them
from it; part of Clifford's horsemen retired to
it; Bruce's baggage-train at Cambuskenneth
Abbey, across the Forth, had actually been
destroyed by some English—but the battle had
still to be fought, and that is what Edward had
come for. The castle was a detail, an occasion.
The English had gone round Bruce's positions,
but could still be beaten. In any case they
had come to insist on an engagement, and
would not remove until some more forcible
argument was presented.

II. *The Scots took the initiative in forcing the
battle.* How could any one, with the texts
before him, come to a different conclusion?
"They tuk the playne," says Barbour; and

[1] *Battle of Bannockburn* (1871), p. 75, note.

historians go on recounting the astonishment of
the King of England without realising that its
whole point lies in this fact. Foot advancing
against horse "In plane hard feild"—that
was the astonishing thing. The phrases of the
other chroniclers carry on the same idea. Of
course this puts aside the properties of bogs
and "pots," and that's the handicap. If the
Scots advanced, such things were not needed;
yet "they marched forward boldly against the
English," says the *Lanercost* chronicler.

Barbour's lengthy analysis of the Scottish
movements depends wholly on this. Descriptions like that of White are mere bold rhetoric:
"It is more probable that, like the rocks of
their own sea-girt land, they firmly awaited the
approach of their foes only to dash them back
like ocean waves broken in a boisterous storm."[1]
It is simply impossible to keep track of such
distortions. Gray says the English passed a
sleepless night in dread of a Scottish attack.
And it is because they pointed the way to
successful attack that the Sunday actions are of

[1] *Battle of Bannockburn*, p. 88.

such cardinal importance: foot, it was shown, could be matched against horse.

III. *In the break-up the English king fled to the castle, a mass of English foot took refuge on the crags, many horsemen were drowned in the Forth and others stifled in crowding over the Bannock where it is affected by the tide.* How is this mass of undisputed fact to be disposed of? Are we asked to believe that the King of England and five hundred horsemen performed what is taken to have been an "impossible" feat and crossed the Scottish front on either flank across the Bannock, or did they ride straight through the Scottish army?

When an army breaks up in flight it breaks up and flies backward, at least it doesn't fly into the arms of its foes. That is welcome not war. If the battle was fought with the Scots between the English and Stirling Castle, more than a mile away, how did the English foot get there? Why did they go there, when they had the whole Scottish lowlands behind them and a straight road home? Why did horsemen, in the same case, ride away to their right, a couple

of miles or so, to get drowned in the Forth?
How was the Bannock so fatal in retreat, so
harmless in the advance? And what were the
Scots doing all the time? These questions wait
for an answer. Mr. Burns flatly declares that
in the retreats to Stirling Barbour, not know-
ing the locality, was blundering: these "two
peculiarities," he says, seem "scarcely to have
attracted the notice of modern writers."[1] They
have been noticed since and accepted, with the
result of giving popular accounts a Gilbertian
flavour: a beaten army flies forward!

But put the battle in the Carse, with the
English extreme right in the direction of
Stirling, the Forth behind and the Bannock to
the left, and the whole debacle is plain and
natural. King, horsemen and foot sheer off to
the castle, that "wes ner" remarks Barbour,
the others go backwards to the Forth or return
over the Bannock as they had come—each part
took the road that seemed to promise safety.
The king and his company didn't venture back
the way they had come, for the Scots were now

[1] *Scottish War of Independence*, ii. pp. 555-6.

there ; they dodged round the New Park behind the field of battle and so eastwards.

These are the essential facts : I suggest that they should be followed to their conclusion, and obscurity will disappear.

IV.

It is possible, perhaps, to catch glimpses of the line of evolution along which the misunderstanding has gone, apart from the fact that, for the early men, some of the material now before us was not accessible. But nothing can excuse neglect of Barbour, and I cannot see any critical advantage in discounting the understanding or equipment of the original authorities.

As soon as we pass the contemporary chroniclers which I have used, we find a disposition to drop the fighting of the first day or to force the two days into one.

Bower in the *Scotichronicon* does this for the fifteenth century. He shows no knowledge of what happened on the Sunday, of Clifford or De Bohun. His account runs to rhetoric, and the rhetoric becomes more abundant in Boece,

who in turn must yield the palm to John Major.
Long speeches appear in the mouths of leaders,
while the topographical and military details
correspondingly shrink. The numbers of the
English swell to three hundred thousand! One
thing may be noted from Boece, to the effect
that when the English "saw thame (the Scots)
rise and cum forthwart, they began to be
affrayit."[1] He is using Barbour. Again he
says the servants came "down the hill, fore-
nence thair enimies."[2] Here then is the first
rising of "Gillies Hill," but what it means is
the hill slope below St. Ninians.

Major puts the Scots in three divisions and
gives the vanguard to Randolph and Douglas,
confounds the engagements of the two days,
and makes Bruce kill "a certain knight" in
personal combat as an opening for the main
engagement. All make great play with the
"pots" under the glamour of Friar Baston's
lines, just the sort of eloquential material they
seem to have liked, and all dabble in ana-

---

[1] Bellenden, edit. 1821, vol. ii. p. 392.
[2] *Ibid.* p. 393.

chronisms—the *Scotichronicon* introducing siege artillery with the English for no earthly reason, and even "bombards" or heavy cannon, Major bringing on "Wild Scots" with the weapons of his own day, and Boece and Major putting the English archers on both wings, a later disposition.

We can now see how George Buchanan compounded his narrative, with its Scots in three divisions, its prominent "pots," its scattered calthrops, archers on the wings, and the killing of de Bohun before the main battle as a thing "small in the telling" (*parvum quidem dictu*), though giving no slight impulse to the result.[1] He supplies the item that the Scots held the left bank of the Bannock, the English the right, and he gives Randolph horsemen to attack Clifford. Buchanan seems to have been utterly ignorant or regardless of Barbour; history is but a literary and political exercise; a mist of rhetoric has settled upon the field.

Now in 1777 the Rev. Mr. Nimmo published

[1] *Rerum Scotic. Historia*, edit. 1762, p. 214.

his *History of Stirlingshire*, and for Bannockburn he turns to Buchanan, of all people, on the
ground that he had special knowledge, "having
long resided at Stirling, when preceptor of
James VI., and had frequent opportunities of
viewing the field."[1] This may cause the up-
holders of what they vainly imagine to be
"tradition" to reflect. Clearly the local his-
torian knew of no "tradition," and what passes
for such is literary stuff of a low order of credi-
bility. Nimmo simply underlines Buchanan,
blunders and all, wherefore he is dismissed by
Lord Hailes, and severely commented upon,
from Barbour, by his editor.

Tytler shows some indecision according to
edition or work, but is also fatally handicapped
in his reliance upon Barbour by apparently
holding to the south position throughout. In
one case he puts it that the Scots, on Monday
morning, after their religious ceremony, "advanced from the higher ground, where they had
first formed their line, into the plain; and the
English, in like manner, came down from their

---

[1] *History*, 2nd edit. 1871, p. 210.

original encampment"; [1] in another it is that
the English, on the night before, "drew off to
the low grounds to the right and rear of their
original position," [2] whence he brings them up
to attack the Scots. Topographically, however,
we are still in the vague, a specific statement is
not made. Even more so with Hill Burton,
though if, as he has it, the battle was fought
where the pitted field caused disaster, and that
was "the tract of flat ground through which an
army might pass to the gate of Stirling Castle," [3]
he may be claimed for the Carse position.
Otherwise he commits himself to nothing
definite.

Professor Oman, who bases a good deal on
the symmetrising Baker, and Sir Herbert Maxwell who, more soundly, gives preference to
Gray, fairly settle on the southern position at
Brock's Brae and the lower end of the New
Park, and so far this is the conception generally
accepted. Sir Herbert Maxwell, using, he tells

[1] *Lives of Scottish Worthies* (1832), ii. p. 39.
[2] *History of Scotland* (edit. 1871), i. p. 268.
[3] *History*, ii. pp. 263, 268.

AN UNWORKABLE PLAN

us, a paper by Sir Evelyn Wood, has constructed
a most detailed presentation of the main conflict
which has convinced many, though, even on its
own terms, it seems to me unworkable. But
it is rather a reflection on Scottish historical
scholarship that an event of such great significance and universal interest should remain in a
nebulous or misunderstood condition, and it is
hoped that, on the eve of the six-hundredth
anniversary, an opportunity will be taken to
arrive at something like general agreement.

INDEX.

INDEX

Ditches, at Loudoun Hill, 48.
Douglas, James, 13, 35 ; character, 37 ; 47, 52-3, 58, 61 ; knighted, 72, 77, 80.
Dupplin Moor, 91.
Dumfries, 11, 14, 61.
Durham, 7.

Easter campaign, an, 21.
Edinburgh, castle, 12, 13, 14 ; city, 47, 53.
Edward I., 1, 3, 9, 10, 17, 19 ; typical army of, 30 ; at Falkirk, 33.
Edward II., 6, 14, 15, 17, 19, 21, 23 ; no soldier, 35, 73 ; forced from field, 83 ; flight, 84.

Falkirk, 44 ; English at, 53 ; battle of, 25, 33, 34, 35.
" Fewall " (Fuel), 40.
Flodden, 14.
Fodder, 15, 16.
Foot, English, 28, 29, 30 ; Irish, 27, 54 ; Scottish, 30, 31, 34 ; Welsh, 27, 30, 35, 54.

Galloway, 2, 4, 11.
Gaveston, Piers, 6, 7.
Geikie, Sir Archibald, 96.
German knights, 26.
Gilbertson, Sir Walter, 88.
" Gillies Hill," 107.
Glasgow, 5.
Gloucester, Earl of, 21, 24, 36, 54, 59, 61 ; suggests delay, 71 ; death of, 75 ; 89, 97.
Gray, Sir Thomas : father, 56, 57 ; son, 66, 101, 103.

Hailes, Lord, 99, 109.
Halidon Hill, 31, 91.
Hereford, Earl of, 21, 36, 54, 59, 75, 87, 90.
Herth, Sir William of, 69.
" Hobbe " King, 3, 8.
" Hobelars " (hobblers), 11, 23, 26.

Irish, 27, 54.

James IV., 14.

Keith, Sir Robert, 53, 78.
King's Park, see New Park.
Knights' fees, 23, 24 ; equipment, 33.

Lanercost Chronicle, 97, 103.
Lang, Andrew, 101.
Lauderdale, 41.
Lennox, Earl of, 43 ; country, 62.
Linlithgow, 5 ; peel, 5, 13, 14, 17.
Lochmaben, 10, 11, 12.
Lothian, 6, 8, 31, 84.
Loudoun Hill, 3, 4, 47, 48.

Macdougalls, the, 4.
Macdouall, Sir Dougal, 11.
Major, John, 107, 108.
Maxwell, Sir Herbert, 95, 97, 101, 110.
Morale, 45, 54, 62, 65.
Moray, Earl of, 32, 37, 46, 51, 52, 56, 57, 58, 59, 61 ; reception, 62, 67 ; attacks, 76-7, 80.

INDEX

MAIN BATTLE

(Advance of Scots and relative positio...